CORPERATE PRENEURS

DISCOVER THE STRATEGIES FOR BUILDING WEALTH WITHIN THE CONFINES OF YOUR WORKPLACE

Dr. Babajide Agunbiade

Corporate Preneurs

Dedication

I would like to dedicate this book to the Duke of Edinburgh International Award Foundation, a charity I support as a world fellow, for their commitment to empowering young people to dream big and impact the world.

Furthermore, I would like to extend a special thank you to my wife, Mrs. Olufunke Agunbiade, for her unwavering support, belief in me, and encouragement. You are my number one fan, and I love you to the moon and back!

"To achieve long-lasting and impactful economic freedom in today's world, it's necessary to think beyond traditional employment. Even if you have a job, you should consider creating your own business."

– **Babajide Agunbiade**

Contents

Acknowledgments

I'd like to express my gratitude to several people who have been a constant source of inspiration and support throughout my journey. Thank you for being with me every step of the way.

I extend my heartfelt thanks to my friends, Mr. Ola Oshe, Mr. Bolaji Olagunju, Mr. Charles Momoh, Mr. Soji Olagunju and Mr. Robert Onyejekwe. Special thanks to Dr. Tony Oguike, who encouraged me to share my experience of achieving success in both my corporate career and personal business.

Meet the Author:
Babajide Agunbiade, Ph.D., FNSE, MBA

Babajide Agunbiade is a renowned Engineer, businessman, and philanthropist with over 25 years of experience in corporate America. He is one of the thirteen globally recognized subject matter experts in subsea production systems. Currently, he serves as the CEO of Alpha Energy Resources, a leading Engineering, Procurement, Construction, and Installation (EPCI) service provider in the Oil and Gas sector of Sub-Saharan Africa.

Agunbiade began his professional career at General Electric (G.E.) and later joined National Oilwell Varco (NOV Inc) where he served as the General Manager for Africa and Golf of Mexico and later as the Director of Business Development for the Subsea Production System business group. During his tenure, he was involved in virtually all the offshore production projects in Sub-Saharan Africa and the Gulf of Mexico, winning over 2 billion USD in offshore production projects.

Before joining NOV, Agunbiade was at various time Principal Engineer at G.E. Gasification and President of G.E. Gasification for West Africa. He led the team that designed the world's largest Integrated Gasification in Combined Cycle (IGCC) plant at Duke Energy's Edwardsport Station in Knox County, Indiana.

Agunbiade is a graduate of the University of Ibadan, where he obtained a combined honors degree in Industrial and Production Engineering. He subsequently attended the GE Edison Advanced Engineering Development Program (EEDP) in Crotonville, N.Y., and earned a master's in systems engineering. He is G.E. green and black belt certified. He holds an MBA from the American Intercontinental University (AIU), a master's degree in organizational management, and a Ph.D. in leadership and business from Higher Place Christian University (HPCU). He is also a Ph.D. scholar in Environmental Policy at Texas Southern University.

Agunbiade's contributions to the oil and gas industry, philanthropy, and social causes have earned him recognition, including the US Certificate of Congressional Award and his appointment as a U.N. Ambassador for Sustainable Development Goals (SDG). He is also a World Fellow at The Duke of Edinburgh's International Award Foundation in London, UK, and a Fellow of The Nigerian Society of Engineers (FNSE).

OTHER AFFILIATIONS:

World Fellow, The Duke of Edinburgh's International Award Foundation, London, UK.

Member, Board of Trustees, International Award for Young People Nigeria (INTAWARD).

Fellow, The Nigerian Society of Engineers (FNSE).

Member, Institute of Industrial & Systems Engineers (IISE).

Fellow, Society of Underwater Technology (SUT).

Member, National Society of Professional Engineers (NSPE).

Member, The Council of Registered Engineers of Nigeria (COREN).

Member, Board of Directors, MobiHealth UK & Dorman Long Engineering Limited.

Patron, Board of Nigerian Union of Journalists, Oyo State, Nigeria.

Chairman, Board of Trustees, The Fiditi Echo.

Patron, Board of Trustees, The Agunbiade Foundation.
Member, Board of Trustees, Fiditi Initiative.

OTHER RECOGNITIONS:

2019 Most Distinguished Alumnus Award, The University of Ibadan.

Recipient, Harris County, Houston, Texas Precinct 1 resolution for contributions to Houston Economy and mentoring.

INTRODUCTION

01

Chapter 1

INTRODUCTION

E volution theorists suggest that only the fittest can survive. This is because, from the onset of humanity, people have had to fiercely compete for access to minimal resources such as food and fire. Thanks to advances in technology and medicine, we've bridged many of our humanity's gaps, helping us survive and thrive in new and exciting ways!

As we mature and navigate the working world, there are essential factors to consider—such as owning a house, improving our health, building meaningful connections with others and ourselves, and contemplating our larger purpose in life.

The Hollywood starlets and business advocates seem to have it all: the fame, money, and lifestyles many of us can only dream of. This visual representation of success and affluence can be a powerful motivator to strive for excellence. Watching the drive and ambition of these successful individuals can inspire and encourage us to tackle our challenges and pursue our dreams!

Does the allure of enticement these celebrities and business moguls present motivate us to work harder and achieve our goals?

Especially when we see people from a similar habitat to ours achieve extravagant success, does that light a fire in you to thrive more, or is it just me?

But I'd ask you to step back from all those worthy resolutions and think about a bigger question: Are you thriving or merely surviving?

Many of us grapple with this critical, lingering question throughout our lives. While survival may be the priority for some in the short term, this way of living can eventually drain our souls and leave us feeling unfulfilled as we ponder on what helps us stay motivated and connected to our purpose.

This question can be challenging, as it requires us to look honestly at our lives and assess whether we are living our best lives.

When we are thriving, we find that we are achieving our goals and making meaningful progress. We feel we control our lives and can make the decisions that best serve our future. We feel fulfilled and content and have a sense of clarity and purpose.

On the other hand, when we are merely surviving, we struggle to make ends meet. We feel like we are constantly trying to catch up and are continually struggling to make it through the day. We feel overwhelmed, insecure, and stuck in a cycle of never getting ahead.

I've been reflecting on this a lot lately and am consciously trying to keep it on my mind as I talk to people and inspire them to do more.

What's the difference between surviving and thriving? Surviving is a grim struggle—you are white-knuckling life, just barely getting by. Surviving is being in a state of constant fear and insecurity, never knowing when the next crisis will hit or how to prepare for it. It is a state of being constantly on guard, never sure when something will go wrong or when the rug will be pulled out from under you. A life of feeling stuck, unable to make meaningful changes or create a better future.

I believe that simply surviving is not enough for myself or my loved ones. Instead, I strive for a life filled with joy, growth, and meaningful experiences. By setting ambitious goals and pursuing our passions, we can create a life that truly fulfills us and brings us happiness.

It is a complex and overwhelming life that can quickly lead to despair and hopelessness. I want more for myself and for those I love. I want a life filled with joy and fulfillment, a life of abundance and contentment, and a life of financial stability and security.

Thriving is living and thinking abundantly. Surviving is a drag, a daily slog to stay alive. Thriving is joyful and infectious. It is a life of feeling secure and confident, allowing one to make meaningful changes and create a better future. If you thrive enough, the road to success can be easily visualized.

Let's be clear: transitioning from surviving to thriving is a far more challenging resolution than joining a gym or deciding to stay consistent in doing yoga. Particularly in times of darkness and difficulty, we must dig deep to channel abundance—or at least the promise of abundance—and rewire our brains. It often seems impossible. Too hard. We might feel ill-equipped, alone, and afraid. And yet, the alternative—merely surviving—is depressing as hell. But sometimes, it's not until we're pushed to the brink that we can truly appreciate the difference.

I've tasted a life of survival, and it's not for me. I refuse to accept that as enough. I hope you will, too.

Our circumstances should not limit the desire to make something of ourselves, so I refuse to accept that barely surviving will be enough for anyone. I believe everyone deserves to reach for their dreams and have the chance to thrive.

You may ask, "But how?"

Simply committing to thriving and leaving behind survival mode is the first and most challenging step. Survival is too often our default; there's comfort in its familiar discomfort. But thriving is not only circumstantial. ("When my life REALLY begins, I'll thrive!"); it's a choice.

Once you reprogram your brain, it's time to clean up the debris left behind—all the survival mode wreckage: bad relationships, unhealthy habits, and a life devoid of intention and purpose.

So, what keeps us from thriving?

The first thing that can keep us from thriving is fear. Fear of failure, fear of the unknown, fear of taking risks – these are all things that can keep us from going after our dreams and reaching our full potential. Fear can boss you around to failure.

Where we cannot ignore the legitimacy of fear, negative thoughts overshadow our thought process. This amalgamation of negative thoughts can blur our vision and prevent us from seeing the need to thrive.

In this state, can one allow oneself to take risks and thrive for betterment?

One of the main things is our inability to open up our minds and take chances. According to the dictionary, to thrive means to gain wealth or possessions. To prosper and flourish. This ultimately boils down to having financial freedom.

Despite this, almost everyone has found a way to adjust to a mediocre lifestyle of surviving by holding on to a job they don't like and paying them way less than they deserve. People who thrive have a strong and secure inner core. They seem to view life as opportunities and challenges they want to engage in and conquer. They are active in their natural gifts and talents. They exercise their passions. The things they love are actuated throughout their life. There is no task in what they love! A few examples can be seen with successful entrepreneurship.

What is so different about them?

Well, the answer is *NOTHING!*

The only difference is that those successful people refused to live their lives paycheck to paycheck. They chose to work for themselves. They sacrificed their present for the better and best possible future.

It is not so difficult if we think about it. Some might disagree. I have found a few keys to the locks of successful entrepreneurship. After risking it all while I was in your shoes, I discovered the keys, doing enough to survive through dusk and dawn. The key to prosperity is multiple stream of income, especially for those who currently have a 9 to 5 job.

Some complain that risking their jobs would bring nothing but debts to their lives. I find their point completely valid. *Who would want to lose a job after years of hustle?* At least the job is paying my bills.

However, not all wishes can be fulfilled with your job—some are even unimaginable.

For instance, do you wish to spend your summers in Hawaii or Bora Bora? Do you wish to travel the world? Do you wish to own a mansion in Beverly Hills? Do you wish to drive the most expensive car?

These wishes might sound unbelievable, but they are the most common and not hard to achieve.

These wishes become nothing but an illusion if you are doing an eight-hour job. I don't think there's a job that provides enough to afford all your dreams and wishes with only an eight-hour job besides being a celebrity or politician.

The average time spent at a job is eight hours a day.

There are still sixteen hours left on your watch. You can utilize your time and effort by trying to build your business.

My emphasis on building your empire imputes grounds for developing independence and control. Believe in your potential and focus on achieving success rather than simply meeting expectations.

Your inheritance won't matter in this regard. You don't have to have a wealthy background to risk initiating a business plan.

You live in a world of digital advancements. The internet has opened up access to various sources of income that don't require answering to a superior. You can directly trade with your clients without needing a boss.

Working for yourself outside of your days job allows you to explore your creativity and take risks without fear of limitations or restrictions. The emergence of platforms like YouTube and TikTok has had a significant global impact, with people earning millions by showcasing their talents. Although it's not typical full-time employment, it can be pursued as a side gig or hustle. Turning your hobbies into a source of income can provide a fun way to make money without feeling burdened. For instance, if you're a passionate cook, you can start your cooking tutorial channel or cater to small events. This can be beneficial in the long run. The longer it takes to settle through, the larger the outcome.

All of this can be done alongside your day job.

You don't have to be like the average American, working enough to meet both ends. To achieve financial freedom, thinking creatively and finding ways to earn extra money that align with your strengths and abilities is essential.

Nowadays, many people create their merchandise, using their creativity and unique styles to succeed in the market and inspire shoppers to purchase. With the advent of e-commerce, trading has become effortless and trouble-free. With their indigenous marketing, compelling consumers towards the goods is no longer challenging.

With this convenience, one can use their portals, websites, and channels to market and sell their products or use such a vendor's medium to sell their products. Social media websites like Facebook, Instagram, and Twitter are being used for business purposes.

Multiple mediums exist to market/channel your products and sell various goods. To succeed, it's crucial to be adaptable and learn from every challenge you encounter along the way.

Before putting your idea into action, it's essential to create a plan and execution strategy to ensure your time and work are managed effectively. If you have a day job, preparing and finding ways to manage your time effectively is essential. With eight hours of work, you are left with sixteen spare hours, of which you spend eight hours sleeping. You are still left with eight hours. You are left with enough time for your side hustle. This will help you save money, providing you with a path to clear your dues/debts? with the extra savings.

The extra amount can help you save money and experience a budget cut by so much. On the other hand, you will find your income expanding day by day.

You can arrange one hour for yourself even if you are busy all day. There are many other ways to make it work.

If you find it hard to find a few hours daily, you must work on your time management and analyze how and where to save time.

Instead of procrastinating, watching TV, and being unproductive, consider finding ways to increase your income. Cutting off cable could free up some extra money and time that you can use to accomplish something outstanding and work towards your goals.

By achieving your financial goals, you can free yourself

from financial constraints and pursue all the dreams you've carried with you since childhood, regardless of how unimaginable they may seem.

Instead of waiting a year for promotions to earn more money, consider creating multiple income streams to help you retire sooner. This way, you can achieve your goals quickly.

All this is possible with careful consideration of time and its management.

The pressure of losing a job can be overwhelming, making you constantly anxious about finding a new one. However, having a side gig can provide a sense of financial security and help alleviate some of that pressure. With a steady source of additional income, you may not even need to consider taking another job and can focus on growing your side gig instead.

Not everyone is fortunate enough to land in high-caliber and limited-positioned jobs. Only some are privileged enough to get hired by good organizations like NASA, Google, Amazon, Apple, Microsoft, etc.

The rest of Americans land an average job, out of which the government extracts a big chunk of their salary as taxation money, which usually leads to debt.

Statistically speaking, 65 million American citizens are carrying debts!

Adjusting and adapting to the sudden change of a side hustle can be depressing and demotivating at some point. Sometimes, you don't get enough of an expected outcome.

"Rome wasn't built in a day," and the same goes for achieving long-term goals. You can't expect results overnight; progress requires patience and persistence. Staying focused on your goals and consistently working towards them over time to see the desired outcome is essential.

This book is my review of the corporate and business world, how I swam across it, how I experienced ups and downs in my career, and how I got myself into starting my own successful business, all while maintaining a high-profile job in corporate America oil and gas, what motivated me, and how I managed time to do everything at the same time, job as well as business.

I have spent 25 years working at the highest level of corporate America while successfully running government procurement, real estate, investments, consultancy businesses, and other business gigs.

This book can provide valuable insights on increasing your wealth and joining the ranks of millionaires. Take advantage of this opportunity and strive to improve your financial situation.

NOTES

26 Ways to Make Money In Your Spare Time With Just Your Phone:

1. Online music reviewer - Sign up on music review platforms (As of December 2023, the average annual pay for a music critic in the United States is $50,596 a year., not bad for a side gig).

2. Survey taker - You can find paid surveys on sites like Swagbucks, Survey Junkie, OneOpinion, Opinion Outpost, Ipsos iSay, MyPoints, and Toluna. (As of December 2023, the average monthly pay for an online survey taker in the United States is $5,383. According to ZipRecruiter).

3. Shopify merchandising -Start, run, and grow your business with Shopify.

4. Micro worker -Work and earn; get offered a micro job for instant and constant payments.

5. Online market researcher via the Field Agent app Twitch streamer.

6. Amazon Direct Publishing Online stock trader.

7. Transcribe online with Scribie Podcaster.

8. Sell items online via Amazon and eBay.

9. Gig Apps such as Steady, Fiverr, TaskRabbit, and Gigwalk for immediate extra income.

10. Get paid to take Branded Surveys via Google Opinion Rewards. Swagbucks. InBoxDollars.

11. CV/Resume writer.

12. Test apps online with UserTesting.

13. Virtual assistant with Fancy Hands app.

14. Review brands with Crowd Tap.

15. Help improve AI with the Appen app.

16. Sign up for Online tutoring with TutorMe, Teachable, Growing Stars Online Tutoring, IXL Official Site.

17. Review commercials and fashion on Slice the Pie.

18. Online research with Clickworker -ClickWorker is a legitimate platform where users can earn money by completing various online tasks, such as data entry, content creation, and research.

19. 19. Audiobook narrator.

20. Forex e-trading via CMC Markets, TD Ameritrade, FOREX.com, City Index, XTB and eToro.

21. Online focus group participant.

22. Website user tester.

23. YouTubing.

24. TikToker.

25. Affiliate marketer.

26. Virtual assistant - become a virtual assistant via websites like Indeed (search for "Remote Virtual Assistant").

In today's world, there is nothing like an unemployed person. What we have are uninformed people. Information is power. Applied information is money. If you need extra income, please put this information into use and go from poverty to prosperity.

THE FOUNDATION

02

Chapter 2

THE FOUNDATION

THE SHACKLES OF CORPORATE LIFE

You eat three times a day to be physically healthy. Won't having three income streams to be financially healthy also make sense? Even if you have a job, having a side income gives you added security. When you get your salary, invest parts of it.

The previous chapter delved into corporate entrepreneurship and its potential to unlock innovation within established organizations. However, before we embark on this exciting journey, it is crucial to understand the foundation upon which corporate entrepreneurship is built. To do so, we must first confront the reality of traditional corporate life and the inherent restrictions imposed by a 9-to-5 job.

For countless individuals, corporate life has become synonymous with the 9-to-5 grind. Day after day, they find themselves confined within the rigid boundaries of office hours, adhering to strict schedules and limited autonomy. The conventional corporate environment often stifles creativity and restrains individuals from exploring their full potential.

The predictable routine of a 9-to-5 job can quickly become suffocating, trapping individuals in a cycle of monotony and unfulfillment. Many people yearn for something more—a greater sense of purpose and the freedom to pursue their passions beyond the confines of a traditional job. It is precisely this desire for more that ignites the flame of corporate entrepreneurship.

The Call for Multiple Income Streams:

- Have a job.
- Have a side hustle.

- Have investments.

- Have real estate.

- Have a gold ETF.

- Have shares.

- Have a mutual fund.

- Have a YouTube channel.

- Have an Amazon KDP account.

- Have treasury bills.

- Have REITS.

- Have life insurance.

Then, if you have money left after all these, you can waste it on posing for social media, lounging in clubs, buying the latest iPhone, wearing designer, etc. Stop going broke because you are trying to look rich! Looking ordinary yet being extraordinarily wealthy is better than looking spectacular but being, in reality, extraordinarily poor.

The limitations of a single income source have become increasingly apparent in a rapidly evolving economy. The traditional notion of relying solely on a paycheck from a 9-to-5 job is no longer a guarantee of financial stability or security. The ever-changing landscape of industries and the rise of automation and artificial intelligence have rendered certain job roles obsolete, leaving individuals vulnerable to sudden job loss or economic downturns.

To thrive in the modern era, individuals must embrace the concept of multiple income streams. Rather than relying solely on a single employer, corporate entrepreneurs understand the importance of diversifying their sources of income. By doing so, they safeguard themselves against unexpected setbacks and create opportunities for exponential growth and financial abundance.

UNLEASHING THE POWER OF MULTIPLE INCOME STREAMS

Breaking the Chains: Embracing Side Hustles

One of the most effective ways to build multiple income streams is by embracing the world of side hustles. A side hustle is an entrepreneurial venture pursued alongside a full-time job, allowing individuals to explore their passions, develop new skills, and generate additional income.

Imagine this scenario: Sarah, a talented graphic designer, works as an in-house designer for a large advertising agency. Although she enjoys her work, Sarah craves the freedom to pursue personal projects and express her creativity beyond the confines of her day job. Recognizing the potential of her skills, she started taking on freelance design projects during her evenings and weekends. Over time, her side hustle gains traction, and she begins attracting clients beyond her network, allowing her to generate a substantial secondary income.

FROM HOBBY TO BUSINESS: THE RISE OF THE GIG ECONOMY

In the age of digital connectivity, the gig economy has witnessed exponential growth, opening up a world of possibilities for those seeking alternative income streams. The gig economy refers to a labor market characterized by the prevalence of short-term contracts, freelance work, and on-demand engagements.

Consider the story of Mark, an aspiring writer who, after years of working a 9-to-5 job in a corporate setting, decides to pursue his passion for writing. He begins by creating a blog sharing his thoughts and expertise on a particular subject. Mark explores opportunities to monetize his writing skills as his content gains traction and his audience grows. He started collaborating with brands as a content creator, ghostwriting for other authors, and even self-publishing his e-books. What was once a hobby soon transforms into a flourishing writing business, providing Mark with creative fulfillment and financial rewards.

INVESTING FOR PASSIVE INCOME: PLANTING SEEDS FOR THE FUTURE

In addition to side hustles and the gig economy, investing represents another powerful avenue for generating multiple income streams. By strategically allocating resources and capitalizing on investment opportunities, individuals can create passive income streams that continue to grow over time.

Consider the example of Oscar, a corporate entrepreneur who has gained financial literacy and an understanding of the power of investments. While maintaining his full-time job, Oscar diligently invests a portion of his income in various assets such as stocks, real estate, and bonds. Over the years, his investments have generated substantial returns, leading to a steady stream of passive income. This newfound financial stability provides Oscar with additional income and allows him to explore new entrepreneurial ventures with reduced financial constraints.

THE DUALITY OF INCOME STREAMS: ACTIVE VS. PASSIVE

In pursuing multiple income streams, it is essential to understand the distinction between active and passive sources of income. Each type offers unique advantages and considerations, providing individuals diverse avenues to generate wealth and financial stability.

ACTIVE INCOME STREAMS: THE FRUITS OF ACTIVE EFFORTS

Active income streams require direct involvement and participation in exchange for monetary compensation. These income streams are typically earned through traditional employment, freelance work, or running a business actively. Active income directly results from your time, effort, skills, and expertise.

For instance, let's revisit Sarah, the graphic designer introduced earlier. While working as an in-house designer for an advertising agency, she receives a fixed salary for her services. This salary represents her active income, as she consistently invests her time and skills in completing assigned projects and fulfilling her role within the organization.

PASSIVE INCOME STREAMS: THE FRUITFUL HARVEST OF INVESTMENTS

Passive income streams, however, allow individuals to earn money with reduced time and effort once the initial setup is complete. Passive income is generated through investments, business ventures, or assets that generate consistent returns without requiring regular active engagement.

To illustrate this, let's consider Michael, the corporate entrepreneur who diligently invests a portion of his income in various assets. One of his investments includes purchasing a rental property. After finding tenants and setting up the property, Michael earns a monthly rental income, representing his passive income. While he may need to handle occasional maintenance or tenant-related issues, the overall revenue is generated passively, allowing him to earn money while focusing on other aspects of his life.

In my own experience, I worked for several years at prominent companies like General Electric (GE). While the stability and structure of a corporate job provided a sense of security, I couldn't ignore the limitations it imposed. My creativity felt stifled within the confines of a rigid hierarchy, and I yearned for more autonomy to pursue my entrepreneurial aspirations.

Eventually, I found myself working in the oil industry, which presented its own set of challenges and opportunities. During this time, I embarked on a side business driven by my passion for business, technology, and innovation. My first side business was registering as a vendor with the State of Texas and the US government to supply procurement items. This was very easy, and I made a lot of money providing basic things such as refrigerators, televisions, sand, household equipment, cars, and so on. From there, I moved into real estate and consultancy. The side business allowed me to explore my creative ideas, develop new skills, and generate additional income beyond my full-time job.

This dual experience—working in the oil industry while nurturing a side business—proved to be transformative. It provided me with a sense of balance, as I could channel my entrepreneurial drive while benefiting from the stability of my corporate role. The additional income generated from my side business brought financial freedom and opened doors to explore my entrepreneurial aspirations further.

In sharing this story, I hope to inspire you, dear reader, to reflect on your journey. You may work within a corporate environment, yearning to break free from the constraints and explore your entrepreneurial side. Consider the potential of multiple income streams, whether through side hustles, investments, or other avenues. Embrace the duality of active and passive income, leveraging both to build a fulfilling and prosperous future.

ONLINE AVENUES OF INCOME

The internet has revolutionized connecting, communicating, and creating opportunities in the digital age. Online platforms have emerged as powerful avenues for individuals to showcase their talents, share their knowledge, and generate income.

TikTok, the popular short-form video platform, has become a breeding ground for creative expression and a source of income for many talented individuals. From dancers to comedians, musicians to artists, TikTok provides a platform for individuals to showcase their skills and gain a loyal following.

One notable example is the rise of influencers on TikTok who have effectively monetized their content. These individuals leverage creativity, unique perspectives, and engaging personalities to amass a substantial following. As their follower base grows, they attract brand partnerships, sponsorships, and opportunities for product endorsements. By consistently producing high-quality content, these influencers transform their TikTok presence into a lucrative income stream.

YouTube, the world's largest video-sharing platform, has created new entrepreneurial opportunities. Content creators across various niches have harnessed the power of YouTube to build engaged audiences, earn ad revenue, and explore additional income streams.

TikTok and YouTube are just two examples of the vast array of online platforms that offer opportunities for individuals to generate income and pursue their passions. From blogging and podcasting to e-commerce and affiliate marketing, the online world provides a virtually limitless landscape for entrepreneurial endeavors.

Whether you have a unique talent, specialized knowledge, or a passion waiting to be shared, consider exploring online avenues to monetize your skills. With dedication, consistency, and a strategic approach, you can build a brand, connect with an audience, and transform your online presence into a reliable and rewarding source of income.

BUILDING THE FUTURE: THE JOURNEY BEGINS

The Catalyst for Change: Embracing Corporate Entrepreneurship

As we conclude this chapter, it is essential to reflect on the transformative power of multiple income streams in the context of corporate entrepreneurship. By embracing side hustles, leveraging the gig economy, and investing for passive income, individuals can break free from the shackles of a 9-to-5 job and unlock a world of possibilities.

As we have explored the world of multiple income streams, the duality of active and passive income, and the power of online platforms, reflecting on your aspirations and potential is crucial.

Inspired by the success stories of individuals leveraging online platforms like TikTok and YouTube, you may be compelled to embark on your entrepreneurial journey. Remember, corporate entrepreneurship is not limited to those working within a specific industry or possessing a particular set of skills. It is a mindset—a willingness to explore, innovate, and create opportunities.

As we move forward in this book, we will delve deeper into the practical strategies, mindset shifts, and frameworks necessary to embrace the path of corporate entrepreneurship. Together, we will navigate the challenges, seize opportunities, and unlock the full potential of multiple income streams.

Corporate entrepreneurship is not merely theoretical but a practical approach to building a more fulfilling and prosperous future. In the subsequent chapters of this book, we will delve deeper into the strategies, mindsets, and frameworks necessary for successfully navigating corporate entrepreneurship

32 Ways To Earn Extra Income to invest in your side hustle and Reduce Cost Today:

1. Earn extra income from Airbnb even if you rent.

2. Minimize restaurant spending by cooking.

3. Earn extra cash by using your social media for affiliate marketing.

4. Earn pocket money by signing up for online survey sites.

5. Restrict online shopping.

6. Protect your wealth from inflation by avoiding banks and investing in ETFs.

7. Protect yourself from currency devaluation by investing in the VOO S&P 500 mutual fund.

8. Lower your car costs by routinely refinancing your auto loan.

9. Protect yourself from recession by investing in a Gold ETF.

10. Substitute Cable with reading.

11. Bundle cable and internet to save 20-40%.

12. Substitute honey with sugar.

13. Substitute beer, wine, and champagne with water.

14. Instead of calling, send an SMS.

15. Instead of clubbing, join a gym.

16. Lower your student loan payments by enrolling in income-driven repayment.

17. Instead of smoking, chew gum.

18. Rather than buying on impulse, go out without your ATM card.

19. Rather than eating out, learn to cook.

20. Rather than physically visiting, video call.

21. Reduce electricity bills by sleeping early, automatically lowering lightbulb usage.

22. Reduce healthcare costs by washing hands as soon as you get home and after shaking hands.

23. Reduce frivolous spending by avoiding parties where you make it rain and wear aso ebi.

24. Lower travel costs by carpooling to and from work.

25. Lower food costs by shopping at street markets instead of fancy supermarkets.

26. Lower billing and requests for loans from friends and family by changing your WhatsApp status to 'I need money!'

27. Learn to cut your hair and save on barbing costs

28. Learn to wash your clothes and save on laundering.

29. Learn to wash your car and cut out car washes.

30. Stock up on household supplies when they're cheap.

31. Wait 48 hours before you click "buy."

32. Stop trying to keep up with the Kardashians.

NOTE

Many people don't understand wealth. They think money is wealth. This is False. Jobs can create money, but they can't create wealth. If you quit or are fired from your job, you stop getting paid. But if you have investments, you don't have to work to get paid. That is wealth! Stop creating money and start creating wealth. Consider how easily money loses value - devaluation, inflation, recession, and government policies affect the value of money. But when these things occur, the value of wealth is recalculated to reflect the current market. Invest in Gold. Nothing on Earth has retained its value since creation, like gold. And nowadays, you don't have to invest in physical gold. You can invest in a Gold ETF. You can also invest in:

- High-yield savings accounts and CDs offer ways to offset the effects of inflation.

- Funds are an affordable way to diversify and invest in bundles of stocks or bonds.

- Government and corporate bonds can provide a source of income and cushion stock market volatility.

NEGOTIATE OR
CREATE A TIME

03

Chapter 3

NEGOTIATE OR CREATE A TIME

Most people do not realize there's no crime in having a side business along with their regular 9-5 job as long as they are not doing this business during their work hours or engaging in a business that directly competes with their current job. In other words, the remaining 16 hours outside your 8-hour workday are yours to use as you wish.

Individuals can engage in a side business alongside their regular 9-5 job without violating labor laws, as long as certain conditions are met.

It's crucial to recognize that modern work-life balance allows for greater flexibility. This means that during your designated 8-hour workday, your primary obligation is to your employer. However, outside of these hours, typically 16 hours a day, you have the autonomy to utilize your time as you see fit, including pursuing personal endeavors such as a side business.

To ensure that you remain within the boundaries of labor laws and employment contracts, consider the following aspects:

1.   Non-compete Agreements:

Some employment contracts might include clauses restricting you from engaging in a business that competes with your employer. It's essential to review these agreements carefully to understand any limitations.

2.   Intellectual Property and Resources:

It's advisable to avoid using your employer's resources, proprietary information, or intellectual property for your side business. Unauthorized use of such assets can lead to legal complications.

3. Conflict of Interest:

Be cautious about situations where your side business interests could clash with your employer's interests. For instance, conducting business with a direct competitor of your employer may raise concerns.

4. Confidentiality and Trade Secrets:

Uphold any confidentiality agreements you have with your employer. This commitment often extends beyond work hours and includes safeguarding trade secrets or sensitive information.

5. Local Labor Laws:

Remember that labor laws and regulations can differ by jurisdiction, so it's advisable to be aware of the specific laws applicable in your area. Consult legal counsel or your HR department if you need more clarification about your rights and obligations.

By adhering to the principles of non-competition, respecting intellectual property, avoiding conflicts of interest, and upholding confidentiality agreements, you can navigate this dual role effectively while remaining within the bounds of labor laws. Always seek professional advice when in doubt to ensure compliance with local regulations.

In certain instances, it may be necessary for an employee to notify the employer that they are starting a business and that business will not be carried out during work hours and does not conflict with the employer's business.

One of the most essential attributes of a successful entrepreneur is your ability to negotiate. Negotiations are ubiquitous and are always present in our daily lives. This is why negotiation skills are crucial and have far-reaching effects on various aspects of our personal and professional interactions.

While seeking multiple streams of income, employees need to maximize their current employment situation by negotiating,

BECOME A NEGOTIATION NINJA

Some people are born negotiators. They have a natural ability to negotiate hard to get what they desire. Some people find it more burdensome and need to practice with more minor negotiations before feeling confident in their ability to battle for what they want.

However, we can practice several negotiating techniques to strengthen our bargaining position and negotiating ability.

1. Form Good Communication:

Observing nonverbal signs and expressing yourself verbally in an engaging way are essential communication skills. Skilled negotiators can adjust their communication methods to suit the audience's needs. Establishing clear communication may prevent misunderstandings that can keep you from reaching a compromise. To form good communication between the parties, it is essential that you first figure out your priorities. Negotiating without determining what outcome you want from the conversation leads to fruitless discussions. Always remember your goal, and then have an honest and direct dialogue. This will build trust and let the other person know of your demands without getting lost due to needing to be more specific.

Another good practice that promotes communication is allowing the other person to provide their point of view. If you don't listen to the other's perspective, it will feel like you're talking to a wall and have no positive outcomes.

2. Practice Active Listening:

Understanding another person's perspective in negotiations requires active listening techniques. Active listening ensures you pay attention and remember precise details without requiring information to be repeated. In contrast, passive listening involves hearing a speaker without taking in their message.

When trying to implement active listening to better your negotiating skills, focus on the facts and do not let your emotions take hold of you. Presenting your argument based on facts makes it much more credible to others.

3. Learn Persuasion:

A crucial negotiation skill is the ability to influence others' opinions. It might assist you in explaining how your suggested solution benefits all parties and persuade others to share your viewpoint. Negotiators should be assertive when necessary and persuasive when possible. You can share your thoughts while still respecting the other side's views if you are assertive.

4. Showcase Problem-Solving and Adaptability:

Recognizing problems and developing timely and appropriate solutions is necessary for successful negotiations. A good negotiator needs to know how a price can be reduced if it's too high. What can be done to raise a resource's availability if it is low? Finding innovative answers to issues could be what makes a successful negotiation.

For a negotiation to be successful, flexibility and adaptability are essential. Every discussion is different, and the circumstances can alter daily. An involved party might, for instance, quickly change its demands. Even though it can be challenging to prepare for every scenario that might arise, a skilled negotiator can swiftly adjust and make a new plan when faced with uncertainty.

5. Manage Your Expectations:

Although you should only go into a negotiation with a goal in mind, it is also pertinent to remember that the other side must also have some goals in mind.

If you feel that both your goals do not align, try to lower your expectations and expect realistic results from any negotiation. Being a skilled negotiator requires striking a balance between being a tough negotiator and a collaborative one. For example, if you want to sell a used piece of machinery, do market research before selling it to understand what it goes for in the market and manage your expectations accordingly.

Your equipment might be a treasured item that sells for much more than it is worth or might need to be more helpful. You will only learn of its importance once you do your research, and only then can you successfully negotiate to get a fair deal for your product.

SEIZE OPPORTUNITIES, MASTER NEGOTIATIONS:

Learning negotiating skills is essential not just for your personal life but also for your professional life. Here are some ways you can improve your life through negotiation skills.

1. Conflict Resolution:

Knowing how to resolve the conflict between both parties by negotiating a deal that benefits them is an art that leads to happy and satisfied customers. You can find a solution that works for both of you instead of settling for less. To the opposition, a composed, professional demeanor will speak loudly. It's crucial to avoid being rash while making decisions. It's best to maintain your composure and have appropriate dialogues that will ultimately lead to advantageous solutions for both of you.

The ideal result is when both parties accept the terms of the negotiation. However, there are many circumstances in which it is difficult to identify a win-win scenario.

Making realistic demands that benefit you and the other party is essential to reaching a conclusion that satisfies everyone. Even though you might want to go all out and be aggressive to close the sale and reap the rewards, this is never the best strategy to use when entering a meeting.

2.   Builds Respect:

Taking everyone into account when participating in the negotiation process is crucial in building relationships.

Respect is not gained by agreeing to everything the other party suggests. However, you can enhance your reputation within your circle if you are a skilled negotiator who understands what is best for the organization. Vendors, clients, and business partners will respect you because they see you as the ideal candidate for the job.

Effective negotiation techniques are crucial in the workplace because they enhance your company's reputation.

People begin to recognize your negotiation skills as you engage in more discussions and get better at them. You can get to a position where your reputation begins to precede you over time.

This will support your future negotiations and enhance the standing of your company.

3. Improves Planning and Strategizing:

If you have refined your negotiation skills, you can enter any deal, conversation, or networking opportunity with the most significant outcome for yourself and your business.

It enables you to negotiate more skillfully and convince people of your point of view more effectively. You can, for instance, use whatever money you save to fund another project or increase your profit margins by taking the time to bargain with a contractor or vendor over the price of a job.

You can use your negotiation skills to bargain with your boss for a wage increase or yearly bonus. It is, in essence, an attitude, and mastering it might provide you with the boost you weren't aware you needed.

4. Boosts Confidence:

Focusing on the issues without caring about the other group or person is a significant component of negotiating. Without this assurance, you put yourself at risk for a deal that benefits everyone but you.

You can make deals that benefit you by presenting information and offering counteroffers while using negotiation skills. If you want to succeed in your next negotiation, be sure you have the poise and assurance essential to deliver.

Any negotiation needs both parties to be confident. When you enter a meaningful negotiation with the confidence that you understand what you're doing, you can concentrate on the deal at hand rather than stressing out whether the other side is outmaneuvering you.

Additionally, it has been demonstrated that more robust agreements happen when a presentation is given with assurance and when offers or counteroffers are made.

5. Raises The Bottom Line:

Getting the best deal for you and your business is the ultimate aim of any negotiation. By doing this, your bottom line will logically improve. For instance, if you successfully negotiate a 10% reduction in your costs, the savings will be applied directly to your profit margin.

Even though some think negotiation benefits one party, it may be advantageous for all parties when done well. The best negotiators can make agreements that benefit both sides in the long run. The ability to negotiate is one that every leader should have. It should be advantageous to both you and the opposition.

CONTRACT CLARITY – ENTREPRENEURS' ROADMAP TO SUCCESS:

It is essential for entrepreneurs working under typical employment contracts to understand the stipulations in their contracts fully. Employment contracts are vital for employers and employees because they stipulate the expectations for both parties. In most cases, there are no implications or restrictions on working on personal projects during non-working hours. This provides entrepreneurs with the freedom to pursue their entrepreneurial endeavors without conflict. Some important things to look out for in your employment contract are as follows:

1. Job Description:

An accurate job description helps keep staff members from feeling overworked or misinformed about what is expected. Although most individuals like detailed job descriptions, a company may prefer a generic one. Without an explicit agreement describing your responsibilities, an employer will have a lot of leeway in claiming that you aren't performing your required duties. If there are any places where you are uncertain, make sure to ask for clarification.

2. Terms:

If the contract contains a term, it is essential to understand the details of the term as well as the reasons for termination before the term expires. Ensure you have a solid understanding of the contract extension options and the grounds for termination.

3. Restrictive Agreements:

Businesses frequently employ restrictive covenants to protect themselves, such as non-compete agreements, no solicitation clauses, confidentiality provisions, and nondisclosure terms.

These covenants try to impose limitations on employees during and after employment. Noncompete agreements are probably the most crucial because they limit an employee's capacity to continue in the same area or launch their firm for a specific time after their employment contract ends.

Find out the compensation that will be given to you during the forced dark period if the contract contains a noncompete clause. If the company does not pay during the allotted time, it is not advisable to accept a position where you cannot work for a prolonged period after quitting the job.

Most jobs don't specify that employees can't pursue other projects in their time, which gives entrepreneurs the liberty to continue the pursuit of their dreams while also being able to sustain themselves financially.

4. Compensation:

The most critical component of every employment contract is the compensation package. A compensation plan frequently covers more than just a salary or biweekly payments.

A complicated bonus or profit-sharing plan may be linked to commission and performance structures. Ensure all extra remuneration, including bonuses and stock awards, is detailed. You should know the performance standards required to qualify for the extra pay. Never accept a response like, "We'll figure it out later."

These are reasons why entrepreneurs need to familiarize themselves with their employment contracts. However, many individuals hesitate to pursue their entrepreneurial interests alongside their regular jobs.

FROM FEAR TO FORTUNE: CONQUER YOUR BUSINESS FEARS:

There are many reasons people still need to learn to start their own business. Some of those reasons are mentioned below:

1.   Uncertain Economy:

The state of "the economy" is one of the most common yet essential concerns people have while beginning a business.

Many would-be business owners feel that if the economy is weak, it must mean it is the worst moment to launch a business.

Every transaction has two sides to it. While specific industries like finance and housing may suffer, others on the other side of the transaction, including foreclosure professionals and storage facilities, may be booming.

This is why caution is essential. It is also important to do market research on your would-be business and figure out its pros and cons before pursuing it.

Unlike a salaried position, business ownership does not come with instant or guaranteed pay. If there is any income, it is proportionate to the business's sales or profits. Trading in your regular paychecks for the unpredictability of business ownership can feel like a giant leap of faith if you've become accustomed to receiving payments on time every payday, regardless of the outcome. It is acceptable to question whether your company can support you and your family.

2. Family Obligation:

People are not only afraid of launching enterprises for financial reasons; many reasons should be considered. Some worry they won't have enough time to spend with their families during a new company's extremely demanding early years. Some people cannot risk such a significant investment as they also have a family to consider. Whether your business idea succeeds or fails, you will still be expected to provide for your family. This is why jumping into a business while being responsible for an entire family is rare.

You can give only so much of yourself; if you work ten or twelve-hour days, you cannot spend the same amount of time at home.

3. Preexisting Debt:

Debt can be a significant barrier to entrepreneurship. You won't be able to get any start-up finance if you have a credit card or student loan debt.

Any revenue your business generates will go straight to your creditors in extreme cases (such as if your wages are being garnished).

This is why being concerned about preexisting debt is a genuine reason to fear starting a business.

Statistically speaking, 65 million American citizens have debt.

Instead of juggling both tasks, focus entirely on repaying your debts before starting a business.

WORK SMART, BUILD DREAMS: UNLOCK ENTREPRENEURIAL SUCCESS:

Entrepreneurship helps people learn how to start working smartly and plan toward retiring early. It is a means to achieve financial independence. Entrepreneurs not only get to strengthen their businesses, but their work also helps develop the economy. Here are some ways entrepreneurship can help you build a successful and fulfilling life:

1.   Autonomy Of Decision-Making:

People with greater job autonomy are more invested and engaged with their work. Entrepreneurs are highly motivated to put in a lot of effort to ensure their organizations succeed because they are in charge of running them. You feel self-governing and self-directing because you suddenly become your boss.

2. Flexible Schedule:

Entrepreneurship allows for that break from the 9 to 5 routine that every individual craves. Although it creates a sense of uncertainty, it also gives you the flexibility to start work at the break of dawn if you're a morning person or late at night if you're a night owl.

Control over your schedule can liberate your mental and physical well-being.

3. An Elevated Standard Of Living:

It is easy to ignore how business owners address social demands and raise the standard of living. Even when those demands and aspirations are rare, they manufacture products and services to satisfy consumer needs. Entrepreneurs fill the needs of every sector.

Any nation's national economy depends heavily on entrepreneurs. Entrepreneurs invest not only their own money but also money from the market. Savings are put to constructive use, becoming a helpful resource.

Entrepreneurs are the backbone of economic wealth development when financial resources are combined. In turn, this results in the production of jobs that advance a nation's economy.

UNLEASH YOUR POTENTIAL: TRANSFORM DOWNTIME INTO PRIME TIME

Utilize your free time effectively. If you invest in your interests, you see your hobbies and passions convert into a source of income, leading to personal and professional growth. Pursuing a personal business alongside a traditional 9-to-5 job can allow individuals to explore their passions while maintaining financial stability. This dual approach is presented as a means to create a fulfilling and purposeful life.

1.   Early To Rise, Ahead Of The Prize:

The proverb "Early bird gets the worm" applies most to business owners. Start the day earlier than you usually do. Start waking up at five if you typically get up at 7. The two extra hours will end up being more valuable than anything else.

That is your quiet time of the day, where you will have

the peace of mind to be present with yourself and reflect on your life to ease your mind of all the worries accumulated in your body throughout the day.

An additional few hours per week amounts to substantial progress over ten years. Pursuing personal business alongside a traditional 9-to-5 job can allow individuals to explore their passions while maintaining financial stability. This dual approach is a means to create a fulfilling and purposeful life.

2. Embrace Lazy Brilliance:

Lazy people are often considered unproductive and the type of people who take a lot of time to get tasks done.

On the contrary, lazy people tend to be more efficient as they develop easier ways to perform jobs that save time, energy, and resources.

If you feel being lazy inhibits your progress, remind yourself that if you can get a job with your lazy attitude, you can also run a successful business and become a time-efficient entrepreneur.

3. Smart Work Trumps Hard Work:

Learning the difference between productivity and efficiency is incredibly important for a successful entrepreneur.

The quantity of your output is your productivity. It is the quantity of work you complete. Contrarily, efficiency revolves entirely around the minimal resources you devote to the job process.

Suppose you have two teams, teams A and B, who are assigned the same task. Team A has two employees, and Team B has five employees. If both teams can complete their work, it indicates that both teams are productive. However, team A is more efficient since they could complete the assigned task with limited resources, i.e., the workforce.

You must be productive and efficient to be a successful entrepreneur or manager. After all, the quantity of your work matters, but the quality and standards you maintain set you apart from the rest.

Innovative Methods to Soothe Employers' Concerns and Boost Efficiency

Recognizing the potential concerns of employers regarding the impact of personal business on productivity is essential to maintaining a balance in your business and your 9 to 5 job.

The following are some strategies for demonstrating commitment, managing time efficiently, and striking a balance between the demands of the job and the entrepreneurial pursuit.

1. Bridging Success: Nurture Workplace Relationships:

Don't burn bridges with your day job once you start your business. The working relationship will be more fruitful and profitable if you communicate well with everyone. Practicing active listening and showcasing empathy will help you establish positive work relationships that might benefit you down the line in your business as well.

2. Make Your Roadmap To Success:

One of your most valuable resources will be time if you manage a small business in addition to your primary employment. To maximize your waking hours, plan your day accordingly.

Create a schedule for your small business at the beginning of each week, considering your social commitments and the requirements of your primary employment.

Remember that doing things for your business when you should be producing for your employer is one of the biggest mistakes you can make when running a business on top of your regular employment. Don't cross the line into using company time or resources for personal benefit because doing so will likely result in your termination.

Similarly, Don't let your day job interfere with the time you should be using to focus on your business. Don't make mistakes such as reading emails from your primary job in the time set aside to concentrate on your project after you've finished your day's work.

3.   Take Constructive Feedback:

This will help you recognize where your peers feel you are lagging, and you will be able to improve yourself.

Your job deserves just as much of your attention as it provides a source of sustenance till your business becomes profitable. Treat your workplace with respect and value its importance in your life.

By stressing the significance of effective time management, we aim to help readers optimize their productivity and avoid wasting valuable free time.

Pursuing personal business alongside a traditional 9-to-5 job can allow individuals to explore their passions while maintaining financial stability. This dual approach is presented as a means to create a fulfilling and purposeful life.

UNLOCKING SUCCESS THROUGH WORK-LIFE BALANCE:

To summarize, this chapter provides practical advice on managing time effectively between a job and a personal business. and creating a work-life balance. Some specific ideas and suggestions to guide readers in starting their entrepreneurial journey are listed below. By advocating for a balanced approach to time management, the chapter aims to support readers in achieving their goals while maintaining a healthy work-life equilibrium:

1. Assess Your Priorities:

The first step in creating a new work-life balance that meets your needs is to take some time to reflect on how the many aspects of your life are affecting one another. Please take a moment to reflect on your present work-life balance and notice your feelings attached to it.

This will help you better analyze and decide what you'd like to change in your life and what you will start focusing on when considering an action plan.

2. Manage Your Time:

It's crucial to learn time management techniques to successfully create a balance between your work and your social life. Humans need social interactions to nourish the soul and replenish happiness and joy.

Examine how you spend your time and, if possible, seek methods to rework your calendar. To focus on one subject at a time, you can "chunk" your time. You can also utilize a matrix method to decide what to prioritize when new duties suddenly arise.

3. Establish Boundaries:

If you find it difficult to say no, try limiting the amount of time you spend working and scheduling time for other activities.

Inform folks of your planned offline times. Go internet-free for a few hours, put your phone aside, and turn off your work emails.

Do you have a helper who could split the workload? Can you let go of the need to be perfect and recognize when good enough is sufficient?

32 Habits That Will Keep You Poor

1. Spending without a budget.
2. Regularly eating out.
3. Buying designer clothes instead of regular ones.
4. Constantly upgrading to the latest iPhone.
5. Driving, taking a taxi/Uber for trek-able trips.
6. Buying lottery tickets/sports betting.

7. Smoking.

8. Doing hard drugs.

9. Alcoholism (different from moderate drinking).

10. Laundering your clothes instead of washing them yourself.

11. Buying on impulse.

12. Buying bottled water instead of a water filterer.

13. Buying things you don't need because they are on sale.

14. Buying coffee or tea at shops instead of making yours at home.

15. Constantly upgrading your electronic gadgets.

16. Overeating.

17. Overgenerosity.

18. Not having a budget and tracking your expenses.

19. Lack of budgeting and/or poor budgeting.

20. Ignoring your debt.

21. Patronising pornographic websites.

22. Borrowing from banks to spend on consumption rather than production.

23. Using credit cards and loans to purchase things you can't afford.

24. Gambling and Falling for Get-Rich-Quick Schemes.

25. Being unclear of your needs, wants, and finances!

26. Buying apps when you can use them for free during a free trial.

27. Womanising.

28. Keeping up with your neighbours.

29. Not paying yourself first (when you get paid, automatically put x amount in savings as opposed to putting in whatever is left at the end of your pay cycle).

30. Using internet data to gossip and idle away rather than to make money.

31. Lending friends money instead of giving them what you can afford. Less than 25% will repay.

32. Avoiding Financial Education.

NOTES

22 Simple Steps To Success

1. Know where you are at.

2. Know where you want to be.

3. Know what you need to get to where you want to be.

4. Know what you don't need to get to where you want to be.

5. Choose thoughts, words, actions, and friends to facilitate #3.

6. Avoid thoughts, words, actions, and friends that detract from #3.

7. Plot your success, not your revenge.

8. Build meaningful relationships.

9. Find good mentors.

10. Invest in knowledge.

11. Avoid procrastination.

12. Take control of your schedule.

13. Learn time management.

14. Eliminate Distractions.

15. Maintain your investments, not your image.

16. Chase hot deals, not hot babes or guys.

17. Dress for success, not to impress.

18. Follow your passion, not the latest fashion.

19. Seek and reward loyalty, not royalty.

20. Achieve success working solo; achieve greatness by working with others.

21. Pray like a Christian and work like a Japanese.

22. Take care of your health.

STARTING A BUSINESS - FROM CONFUSION TO CLARITY

04

Chapter 4

STARTING A BUSINESS – FROM CONFUSION TO CLARITY

▬▬▬

Many people are intimidated by the thought of starting a business as they don't understand the different types of businesses and cannot determine which category their business venture will fall in. To guide aspiring entrepreneurs in their journey, we outline essential steps laying the foundation for a successful business venture.

We will address common misconceptions and guide

you to help you navigate the initial stages of starting a business. We will discuss the common factors that incite fear in entrepreneurs and hold them back from unlocking their potential.

FEARS OF ENTREPRENEURIAL ILLUSIONS:

1. The Fear Of Failure:

The fear of failure is one of the most prevalent fears among people who want to start their businesses. This fear can be caused by several things, such as a lack of confidence in one's skills, fear of rejection, or worry about failing to live up to others' expectations.

Focusing on the advantages rather than the drawback of establishing a business is the key to overcoming this fear. It's crucial to remember that failure is a normal part of the business process and that even the most successful business owners have occasionally failed. Concentrating on the potential for success rather than the likelihood of failure is crucial. Having a plan is one approach to doing this.

2.   Fear Of Responsibility:

Being in charge of your livelihood as a business owner can be frightening. Knowing that you are solely responsible for fulfilling your needs without a steady monthly income is daunting. However, there comes a time in an entrepreneur's life when you become in charge of providing for the livelihoods of your employees.

That's a lot of responsibility, which can understandably cause some anxiety in business owners. But with careful planning and wise choices, you can manage it. Establish short-term revenue objectives so you can make necessary changes to stay on course. Recognize the costs of adding a new employee, considering benefits and other expenses.

3.   Fear Of Debt:

The personality of an entrepreneur is perfectly encapsulated as a person who takes unusually high financial risks to try to run an organization.

Investing in your business is a nerve-wracking ordeal, which requires a lot of trust in yourself and your ability to make a business successful. If you invest in your business and don't see an instant result, keep working on it and put in your hard work to convert it into a successful venture. You won't ever make a profit if you give up before making one.

Funding a new business is complex, and costs frequently exceed your projected budget. It might be challenging to distinguish between investing more to overcome a hurdle and wasting good money on poor choices.

If you're considering taking out a loan for your company, try asking yourself: Do I need this money to support an unproven product or service, or can I use it to expand my existing successful company? If the latter, you might want to consider other areas where you can make savings. If you're taking on debt to expand your business, it may be a wise decision, and you should get over your debt-related fear in that circumstance.

However, if you feel like your company won't turn a profit, remind yourself that you have already made back the investment from the business. This keeps the option of abandoning the business open if necessary. Even though you should trust your business's success, an entrepreneur knows when to abandon a sinking ship to prevent drowning with a problematic business idea.

Remember, all your business ventures are merely ideas until you decide to act on them. This is why the true value lies in the entrepreneur and not the product.

4. Fear Of Competition:

You might benefit from a first-mover advantage if your product or service is unique. However, as soon as another business learns about your offering, they will try to imitate it or develop a different product that offers customers the same relief. Recognizing that competition confirms your idea will help you overcome this fear. The benefit of competition is that it can broaden the consumer "pie," which expands the market and boosts profits for all participants.

5.   Fear Of Lack Of Knowledge:

Lacking the knowledge or expertise necessary to launch their firm is another fear that keeps people from becoming entrepreneurs.

While some might think that starting a business requires a bachelor's in administration (or a closely comparable field of study), that isn't necessarily the case.

The best ways to build businesses are through trial, error, and practical application. As you develop, explore, take cautious chances, and discover what works best for the business you're attempting to establish, you always learn new things and gain the knowledge you would never be able to without hands-on experience.

PRODUCT VS. SERVICE - CHOOSING THE RIGHT FOCUS

Starting a business requires making a critical decision: whether to offer products or services.

Product-based companies are those that create and sell

tangible goods. These goods are typically produced in a factory, delivered to a location, and then supplied by the business to its customers. On the other hand, service-based companies provide intangible value through their expertise, skills, and time.

There are many factors to consider when deciding whether to start a product-based or service-based business. For example, product-based companies will require significant capital to start, as they often need to invest in equipment and inventory.

On the other hand, service-based companies may require fewer upfront investments but more time and effort to build a reputation and customer base.

While both options have their merits, selling products can provide unique advantages. Products often offer scalability, as they can be manufactured or sourced in larger quantities, allowing for potential growth and increased revenue.

Some key features that make product-based businesses sound more enticing to entrepreneurs are as follows:

1. Creativity:

Instead of focusing on your client's needs, you have the opportunity in a product-based business to let your invention drive your output. You can align yourself with the company's vision and give yourself the freedom to build an innovative product by exercising creativity.

On the other hand, in a service-based business, you are working for someone, and your decisions will be in respect to their demands, thus somewhat inhibiting your creative ideas.

2. Scalability And Revenue Generation:

In a product-based business, once the product is created, the production is easy and doesn't require an increase in employees or office space, saving you further expenses.

Similarly, you can increase the revenue of your products tenfold with the help of a marketing team, which can increase your sales and market value.

On the other hand, if your company provides a service

that bills clients hourly for services or project-based work, then billable hours directly affect your revenue. To expand your business and provide additional services, you must expand your workforce, thus increasing your cost.

3. Customer Service:

In a product-based business, it is pertinent to remember that your customers are the reason your business is booming. A satisfied customer base ensures a successful business. Although the type of customer service is strongly related to the product, it still varies greatly.

These considerations are essential because your customers keep your business afloat. Although it will take time, and on occasion, you will need to be able to handle the rush of clients, building a positive relationship with your clientele will benefit you in the long run.

On the other hand, in a service-based business, you spend a lot of time coordinating and managing the number of clients, their phone calls, emails, and other methods of connecting with customers. These factors lead to low performance and eat-up time that could be spent on other crucial duties.

Products can also have higher profit margins than services, as they can be priced based on production costs and market demand.

Furthermore, selling products can lead to repeat sales and customer loyalty, fostering a more sustainable business model. However, it's essential to carefully consider your specific industry, target market, and personal interests before making a final decision.

STEPS TO START A SUCCESSFUL BUSINESS:

1. Create a Business Plan:

The first step in starting a successful business is a well-crafted business plan. It serves as a roadmap for your entrepreneurial journey and outlines your objectives, target market, competitive analysis, marketing strategies, financial projections, and more. Take the time to research and write an inclusive business plan to clarify your vision and attract potential investors.

2. Assess Your Finances:

Before launching your business, assessing your finances and determining how much capital you can invest is crucial. Consider your savings, assets, and potential funding sources, such as loans or investments from partners or family members. A realistic understanding of your financial situation will guide your decision-making process and ensure you have the necessary resources to support your business in the early stages.

3. Decide Where to Invest:

Once you have assessed your finances, carefully consider how to invest your money in a way that is the most profitable to your business. Invest in supplies that will last you for a long time; the initial investment in a business should be utilized to buy the pricey essential equipment that will last you for some time. This decision may involve purchasing inventory, equipment, or software, leasing office or retail space, investing in marketing efforts, or hiring professionals to assist with specific tasks. Prioritize investments that will directly contribute to the growth and success of your business.

4. Form an LLC:

Forming a legal entity like a Limited Liability Company (LLC) is often advisable to protect your assets and limit liability. An LLC separates your personal and business finances, protecting your assets in the event of legal action or bankruptcy. Consult with an attorney or business advisor to understand the requirements and benefits of different business structures and determine the best fit for your venture.

5. Establish Trust:

Building trust with your customers and clients is essential for long-term success. Consider establishing trust elements such as professional certifications, testimonials, guarantees, or partnerships with reputable organizations. Showing your customers you are trustworthy through consistently good results and certifications from reputable organizations in your field will help you establish a dedicated customer base.

6. Get Your Business Insured:

Protecting your business from unexpected risks and liabilities is crucial. Acquire the necessary insurance policies, such as general liability insurance, professional liability insurance, property insurance, or workers' compensation insurance, depending on the nature of your business. Consult an insurance professional to determine the appropriate coverage for your needs.

7. Build a Team:

As your business grows, you will likely need assistance to manage various aspects of your operations. Identify critical positions that require expertise and consider hiring employees or collaborating with freelancers or contractors. Define roles and responsibilities clearly to ensure smooth functioning and productivity within your team.

8. Find Vendors:

Establishing relationships with reliable vendors is essential to deliver high-quality products or services. Conduct thorough research to locate vendors who offer competitive pricing, timely delivery, and consistent quality.

Forming partnerships based on trust, open communication, and shared goals will help both businesses flourish.

UNDERSTANDING DIFFERENT BUSINESS STRUCTURES:

There are several business structures, each with advantages and considerations. Knowing different structures of businesses opens entrepreneurs' eyes to the vast arena of business ownership. It helps them develop the best possible plan of action that aligns with their business goals.

Some common options include:

1. Sole Proprietorship:

A sole proprietorship is the simplest business structure, where you are the sole owner and operator of the business. While it offers complete control, it also exposes you to personal liability for business debts and legal issues.

2. Partnership:

Partnerships involve two or more individuals sharing ownership and responsibilities. General partnerships distribute profits and liabilities evenly, while limited partnerships offer limited liability to some partners.

Carefully consider partnership agreements and legal advice to ensure clarity and protection for all parties involved.

3. Corporation:

A corporation is a separate legal entity from its owners, providing limited liability and potential tax advantages. Corporations require more formalities and regulations, including appointing directors and shareholders and adhering to corporate bylaws. Due to these reasons, most entrepreneurs don't opt for a corporation, as their initial business plan isn't large-scale enough to afford directors, or many employees for that matter. Successful startups grow and become corporations, but few start as corporations due to limited funds.

4. Cooperative:

We briefly discuss the cooperative structure, where individuals or businesses with common goals pool resources and share ownership and decision-making. It is a democratic form of business ownership. Co-ops are democratically controlled by their member-owners, and unlike a traditional business, each member gets a say in how the business is run. Services or goods provided by the co-op benefit and serve the member-owners.

5. Limited Liability Company (LLC):

The LLC structure combines elements of both partnerships and corporations. It is a type of corporate structure that shields its owners from being held personally liable for the firm's obligations. Limited liability companies are hybrid legal entities with traits shared by corporations, partnerships, and sole proprietorships.

The provision of flow-through taxes to the members of an LLC is a feature of a partnership rather than an LLC. However, the limited liability aspect is similar to that of a corporation.

These are just a few examples; other business structures, such as Limited Partnerships (LPs), are available. Consult with a business attorney or advisor to determine the most suitable structure for your business goals and circumstances.

Starting a business can be a complex and daunting process, but with the correct information and approach, you can navigate the initial stages successfully.

By understanding the advantages of selling products over services and taking essential steps like creating a business plan, assessing your finances, forming a legal entity, and building a trusted team, you can establish a solid foundation for your venture.

Additionally, exploring different business structures will allow you to choose the option that aligns with your goals and provides the necessary legal protection. Knowing about the type of business you're getting into not only helps you build it accordingly but also helps you better understand the legal procedures and the tax brackets your business will be categorized into.

With careful planning and meticulous implementation, you can transform confusion into clarity and establish a thriving business that will take you on a rewarding entrepreneurial journey.

NOTES

The word 'work' is very deceptive. It makes you think work must be laborious. This is absolutely False! Beyonce works when she sings. Venus Williams works while she plays tennis. Warren Buffet works when he makes investments. Gordon Ramsay works when he comes up with cooking recipes. 12-year-old Ryan Kaji works when he plays with toys and earns $22 million annually from his YouTube channel. And a laborer also works when he lifts cement.

Work and play can coexist. Work has to be productive. It does NOT have to be laborious!

BUSINESS PLAN

05

Chapter 5

BUSINESS PLAN

When starting a business, there are many aspects to consider, your finances being the top priority. Here are some steps to help you navigate the financial aspects of your business:

1. Explore Sustainable Methods of Funding your Business:

Investing all of your resources in one project is never a wise plan. You have a higher chance of obtaining suitable funding that matches your particular needs when you diversify your sources of financing.

Remember that banks do not consider themselves your exclusive source of funding. As a business owner seeking investment, you must be a proactive and resourceful entrepreneur. One way to achieve this is by researching and considering alternative forms of funding in addition to traditional sources. By showing investors that you have explored these options, you can demonstrate your commitment to finding innovative ways to grow your business.

You can also seek investors or use your savings to fund your business. This gives you more control and flexibility over your finances in the early stages.

Determining the most suitable option depends on various factors, such as the stage of your business, industry, financial needs, and personal preferences. Here are some standard methods for acquiring funding:

a.   Personal Savings:

Investing your money into the business is often the first step for many entrepreneurs. It demonstrates your commitment and may make attracting other investors or lenders easier.

b. Friends and Family:

You can approach friends or family members willing to invest in your business. Establish clear terms and formalize the agreement to avoid potential conflicts.

c. Angel Investors:

Angel investors are individuals or groups who provide capital to startups in exchange for equity. They often offer expertise, industry connections, mentorship, and funding.

d. Crowdfunding:

Platforms like Kickstarter, Indiegogo, and GoFundMe allow you to raise funds from many people who contribute more diminutive amounts. It's essential to have a compelling pitch and attractive rewards to motivate backers.

e. Loans/ Grants:

You can approach banks and other financial institutions for a business loan. They usually require a solid business plan, collateral, and credit history. The U.S. Small Business Administration offers various loan programs to support small businesses. These loans typically have more favorable terms and lower interest rates than traditional bank loans.

You can also research and apply for grants from government agencies, nonprofit organizations, or foundations. Grants are often available for specific industries, research and development, or social initiatives.

Remember that each funding option has pros and cons, and it's crucial to carefully evaluate the terms, obligations, and potential impact on your ownership and control of the business before proceeding.

Consulting with a financial advisor or business mentor can also provide valuable insights and guidance to determine the appropriate funding source for your business model.

2. Understand And Develop Thorough Financial Statements:

Understanding and developing your financial statements, including the income, balance, and cash flow statements is crucial. These statements provide a snapshot of your business's financial health and help you track revenues, expenses, assets, and liabilities.

Investors are more inclined to invest in your business if you have updated financial statements of all your expenses.

There are three main types of financial statements: The balance sheet, the income statement, and the cash flow statement.

When you know how to read your financial statements, you can find ways to make more profit, expand your business, or catch problems before they grow.

3. Find your Unique Selling Proposition (USP):

Identifying and clearly defining your product's unique selling point helps you understand what sets it apart from competitors and how it addresses customers' needs or solves their problems. This knowledge will help you craft effective marketing strategies and set appropriate pricing.

Instead of supporting everything, businesses with USPs identify and align with one specific goal, and it becomes a defining feature for the company. You can find your USP by analyzing the strengths and weaknesses of your company and applying the following techniques for your business.

4.   Understand The Demands Of Your Audience:

Brainstorm the factors that motivate your customers to buy the product. Try to look for more profound reasons other than ample supply, as your competitors can easily replicate that.

5.   Analyze Your Competitors On These Criteria:

Try to determine your competitors' USPs to understand their client base. This will help you understand your business's clientele and make decisions catering to their needs.

6.   Utilize Your USP:

The final thing is to protect your USP after you identify it. You should expect your competitors to steal any different idea that increases your sales and be prepared to defend it. For example, if your business offers a new feature to its clients, expect your competitors to introduce a similar feature soon. Be prepared to adapt and improvise to make your business unique and focus on building on your USP.

7.   Determine Appropriate Selling Platforms:

Decide on the platforms where you'll sell your products or services. This could include e-commerce websites, online marketplaces, brick-and-mortar stores, or a combination of these channels. When selecting the platforms, consider the target audience, competition, and convenience factors. Here's a step-by-step guide to help you make an informed decision:

a.   Define Your Target Audience:

Start by identifying your ideal customers. Consider their demographics, preferences, and online behavior. Are they active on social media platforms, prefer shopping on e-commerce websites, or frequent niche marketplaces?

b.   Research Available Platforms:

Explore various selling platforms and marketplaces to see which ones align with your target audience. Consider both general e-commerce platforms and specialized niche marketplaces.

c.   Consider Platform Fees And Policies:

Understand the fee structures of different platforms, including listing fees, transaction fees, monthly subscriptions, and any other charges.

Review the platform's policies regarding returns, refunds, seller protection, and customer disputes to ensure they align with your business practices.

d.   Analyze Competition:

Research your competitors and see which platforms they are using successfully. Analyzing their presence and customer engagement on different platforms can provide insights into where your target audience will likely be active.

e.   Assess Platform Reach And Traffic:

Evaluate the reach and traffic of each platform. Consider the number of active users, monthly visitors, and geographical distribution. A more extensive user base and high-traffic platform can offer more exposure and sales opportunities.

After deciding on suitable platforms for your business, continuously monitor your performance on different platforms and adapt your strategy accordingly. If specific platforms are generating little results, consider exploring new ones or reallocating your resources to more successful channels.

Remember, it's not necessary to be present on every available platform. Instead, focus on platforms that align with your target audience, offer the right features, and provide a positive selling experience for your business.

8.   Set Revenue And Gross Margin Objectives:

Determine your revenue goals and establish realistic gross margin targets. Revenue objectives define the total income you aim to generate, while gross margin objectives show the profitability of your products or services after deducting the cost of goods sold. Set these objectives based on market research, cost analysis, and your business's growth strategy.

Here is a straightforward approach to determining revenue goals and establishing realistic gross margin targets:

a.   Market Research:

Conduct a thorough analysis of your target market, including its size, growth rate, trends, and competitive landscape.

Identify the pricing dynamics in the market, including the price sensitivity of customers, competitor pricing strategies, and the perceived value of your products or services.

b.   Cost Analysis:

Determine the cost of goods sold (COGS) for each product or service you offer. This should include direct costs (materials, labor, etc.) and indirect costs (overhead, administrative expenses, etc.). Then, calculate the gross margin for each product or service by subtracting the COGS from the selling price.

Now, analyze the cost structure and identify areas where cost optimization or efficiency improvements are possible.

c.   Business Growth Strategy:

Define your business's growth strategy, considering market penetration, expansion, product development, or diversification.

Evaluate the potential impact of your growth strategy on revenue and gross margin. For example, launching new products might increase revenue but could involve higher production costs initially.

9.   Set Revenue Objectives:

Based on market research and your growth strategy, determine the total income you aim to generate. This can be an annual, quarterly, or monthly target.

Consider market share, customer acquisition and retention rates, and expected sales growth to determine achievable revenue goals. Analyze the gross margin achieved by your competitors or industry benchmarks to understand the acceptable range for your business. Consider factors such as economies of scale, pricing strategies, and product differentiation to define realistic gross margin targets. Consider any necessary adjustments based on your cost analysis and the desired profitability of your business.

10. Monitor and Adjust:

After setting revenue goals, it is crucial to continuously monitor your revenue and gross margin performance against the established objectives. Regularly reviewing market conditions, cost structures, and competitive landscape to make any necessary adjustments to your objectives will help you take charge of a changing market and pave your way.

Revenue and gross margin objectives should be challenging yet attainable. Setting overly ambitious targets may lead to unrealistic expectations or compromise other aspects of your business. Regular evaluation and adjustment of your objectives based on market dynamics and internal capabilities are crucial for long-term success.

These steps provide a foundation for your financial planning, but many other considerations are involved in running a successful business. Seek professional advice if needed, continuously monitor and adapt your financial strategies, and stay informed about industry trends to maximize your chances of success.

NOTES

Both wealth and poverty are mindsets. The poor think of how to spend money, while the rich focus on how to make money. Give a poor man one million dollars; if he does not change his way of thinking, he will become poor again. Wealth is the mentality, not the money. The secret to wealth, therefore, is to avoid associating with people with a consumer mentality. Not because you hate them but because you tend to become like those you associate with. Befriend those you want to be like and mentor those who want to be like you. Finally, remember that "wealth does not like people who want to be wealthy". Wealth loves people who work to be wealthy. Never forget that!

MARKETING MASTERPLAN

06

Chapter 6
MARKETING MASTERPLAN

M arketing is critical in the success and expansion of a small business and a startup. It implies different activities that aim to promote products or services, establish brand recognition, attract customers, and generate sales.

Here are some fundamental reasons why marketing holds significance for a business:

1.   Enhancing Brand Visibility:

Through effective marketing strategies, businesses can

create and strengthen their brand identity, making it easily recognizable and memorable for consumers.

Consistent brand exposure across different marketing channels, such as advertising, social media, and content creation, helps build brand recognition and sets it apart from competitors.

A great example of this is Coca-Cola. It is a globally renowned brand. Their continuous marketing efforts, including iconic advertising campaigns and event sponsorships, have led to strong brand recognition and association with soft drinks. Even now, when they are a household name, their renewed efforts toward brand visibility help maintain their position in the market.

2. Generating Leads And Sales:

Marketing activities are designed to attract and convert potential customers into paying customers. By utilizing persuasive tactics, businesses can influence consumer behavior and drive sales.

Marketing campaigns often include promotions,

discounts, product demonstrations, and other strategies encouraging purchases.

Apple's product launches and marketing campaigns create anticipation and excitement at every launch, resulting in long queues outside their stores and high sales volumes for new products.

3. Cultivating Customer Loyalty:

Effective marketing not only helps in attracting new customers but also fosters customer loyalty. Businesses can establish long-term customer relationships by providing a positive customer experience and consistently delivering value, leading to repeat purchases and positive word-of-mouth recommendations.

Starbucks employs a loyalty program that rewards customers with points for each purchase, offering incentives like free drinks or exclusive offers. This marketing strategy is an excellent example of how they encourage customer loyalty, which drives repeat business and ensures customer retention.

4. Expanding Market Reach:

Marketing enables businesses to reach a broader audience and tap into new market segments. Businesses can tailor their messages to specific demographics or geographical regions through targeted marketing campaigns, expanding their customer base and market share.

For example, Airbnb has utilized targeted marketing to reach diverse audiences, including families, business travelers, and adventure enthusiasts. Their marketing efforts showcase unique accommodations and experiences to attract various customer bases.

5. Adapting To Evolving Customer Needs:

Researching and analyzing your consumer patterns provides valuable insights into customer preferences, behavior, and market trends. By staying informed about customer needs and market dynamics, businesses can adjust their strategies and offerings to remain relevant and competitive.

A great example is how Netflix analyzes viewer data to personalize recommendations and develop original content that caters to specific audience segments, ultimately enhancing the customer experience.

A well-executed marketing strategy is vital for businesses as it plays a pivotal role in establishing brand recognition, attracting customers, boosting sales, fostering loyalty, adapting to market changes, and gaining a competitive edge.

In today's fiercely competitive business environment, marketing is an indispensable function that enables businesses to flourish and grow. Therefore, it is imperative to comprehend and formulate a comprehensive marketing plan to ensure the success of your business.

MARKETING PLAN: A PROFIT PROPELLER

A marketing plan is a carefully curated document that describes an organization's objectives, techniques, and actions to market its offerings effectively. It guides the marketing team, offering a comprehensive outlook on how the organization plans to connect with its desired audience, generate potential customers, enhance brand recognition, and boost sales and profits.

A thoroughly constructed marketing plan usually consists of the following essential elements:

1. Analyze your Current Situation:

This concisely overviews the marketing plan, highlighting the main objectives and strategies. Take a comprehensive look at your business, including your offerings, strengths, weaknesses, and available resources.

This involves thoroughly assessing internal and external factors impacting the organization's marketing efforts. It includes analyzing the company's strengths, weaknesses, opportunities, and threats and evaluating the competitive landscape and target market characteristics.

Nike, a renowned sportswear brand, regularly assesses its current situation to stay competitive. They analyze their product offerings, strengths (e.g., strong brand recognition), weaknesses (e.g., high production costs), and available resources. They also examine market trends, customer behavior, and industry developments to identify opportunities and threats.

2.   Analyze your competitors:

Conduct thorough research on your competitors to gain insights into their strategies, strengths, weaknesses, and market positioning. Identify what distinguishes your business and find ways to leverage those unique qualities.

Additionally, it analyzes market trends, customer behavior, and industry developments. For example, Coca-Cola, a leading beverage company, conducts extensive competitor research. They analyze the strategies, strengths, and weaknesses of other beverage companies like PepsiCo and Dr. Pepper Snapple Group. Coca-Cola identifies what sets the company apart, such as its iconic brand, extensive distribution network, and innovative marketing campaigns.

3.   Identify Your Target Audience:

Try to identify the specific market segments that your business aims to target. This includes the target audience's demographic, psychographic, and behavioral attributes, aiding in refining marketing messages and tailoring campaigns accordingly. This information will help you tailor your marketing messages and select the most appropriate channels to reach them.

Dove, a personal care brand, defines its target audience as women who value authenticity and inclusivity. They create detailed buyer personas, considering age, body image concerns, and purchasing behavior. Dove tailors its marketing messages to empower women and challenge beauty stereotypes.

4. Marketing Objectives:

Establish clear marketing objectives that align with your overall business goals. These objectives should align with the overall business goals and may include increasing market share, improving brand recognition, expanding into new markets, or launching new products.

Ensure these objectives are measurable and attainable within a specific timeline. For example, you might aim to increase sales by 20% in the next three months or generate 500 leads per month.

5. Determine Pricing And Positioning:

Conduct market research, analyze costs, and consider the perceived value of your offerings to establish a pricing strategy. Differentiate your product or service from competitors and ensure it resonates with your target audience. Communicate the unique value you provide.

The marketing plan includes a detailed budget outlining the expected costs of executing the tactics. It specifies how funds are allocated to different marketing activities, ensuring efficient utilization of resources.

Tesla, an electric vehicle manufacturer, establishes a pricing strategy that reflects the value of its products. It conducts market research, considering factors such as production costs, battery technology advancements, and the perceived value of sustainable transportation. Tesla positions itself as a premium brand, differentiating itself from traditional automakers and emphasizing the environmental benefits of electric vehicles.

6. Create A Detailed Action Plan:

Develop a comprehensive action plan that outlines

specific marketing activities necessary to implement your strategy. Assign responsibilities, set timelines, and allocate resources for each activity. This may involve advertising campaigns, content creation, social media engagement, events, or partnerships.

Include details such as the marketing channels to be used (e.g., digital advertising, content marketing, email campaigns), budget allocation for each tactic, and the timeline for execution.

Red Bull, an energy drink brand, developed a comprehensive action plan for its marketing efforts. They allocated resources for activities like extreme sports sponsorships, content creation (e.g., Red Bull TV), and targeted social media campaigns. Red Bull collaborates with athletes, organizes events, and partners with influencers to engage its target audience and build brand loyalty.

7. Monitor and Improve:

Establish key performance indicators (KPIs) to track the effectiveness of your marketing efforts. Regularly monitor and evaluate these KPIs to measure the success of your marketing plan. Identify areas for improvement and make necessary adjustments to optimize your results.

This enables ongoing monitoring, analysis, and adjustment of marketing strategies based on real-time data. A straightforward implementation timeline that outlines specific milestones, deadlines, and responsible parties for each activity helps ensure accountability and keeps the marketing team on track.

Google, for example, uses measure metrics like click-through rates, conversion rates, and customer acquisition costs. Based on the results, Google continually adjusts its marketing strategies, optimizing its advertising campaigns and user experiences.

Overall, a marketing plan serves as a comprehensive guide for organizations to strategically approach their marketing efforts, aligning them with business goals and maximizing the effectiveness of marketing campaigns. It provides a framework for decision-making, resource allocation, and continuous evaluation and improvement of marketing activities.

NOTE

It's important to discover your strengths early on in life. Nobody is good at everything, so figuring out what you excel at is crucial. If you don't take the time to identify your strengths, you'll be judged by your weaknesses, which can lead to failure and damage your confidence. Don't wait for others to tell you what you're good at; take control of the process and find out for yourself. Once you know your strengths, use them to achieve your goals and make your mark on the world.

JUGGLING YOUR CAREER AND GROWING YOUR BUSINESS

07

Chapter 7

JUGGLING YOUR CAREER AND GROWING YOUR BUSINESS

S tartups signify new beginnings and allow people to explore their abilities as business owners. Although a well-settled business is an excellent source of income and can bring great prosperity, starting a business as an entrepreneur is far from glamorous and brings a lot of uncertainty.

This is why many individuals choose to maintain a day job as they run a business alongside it, ensuring a paycheck to pay their bills while saving the money from the business for further investment. Some people establish small businesses to earn extra money to save for vacations while utilizing their paychecks from their day jobs to pay for monthly expenses.

Whatever the reason for starting a business, every individual should try starting a business at least once. Life is too short to think about the what ifs; you should try to run a business while establishing safety measures to fall back on in case of failure. As they say, "Hope for the best, prepare for the worst."

Creating a business that requires minimal upkeep and can be managed alongside your day job is an excellent way to generate extra income while maintaining regular employment. Here are some steps to help you get started:

SIDE HUSTLE SUCCESS: CREATE A BUSINESS ALONGSIDE YOUR JOB:

In this growing inflation, a single source of income often feels constricting, and many people turn to techniques to diversify their revenue streams and explore new opportunities that align with their interests and aspirations.

If you want to expand your business and find more financial independence by creating a low-maintenance business that seamlessly integrates with your regular employment, try to implement the following points in your life:

1. Minimize Time Commitment; Choose a Low-Maintenance Business Model:

Select a business model that doesn't demand constant attention or a significant time commitment. Avoid ventures that require physical storefronts, extensive inventory management, or a high level of customer interaction.

For example, an online drop shipping business or a content-based website generates passive income through advertising. This doesn't require much investment and requires little time commitment.

2. Embrace Scalable Ideas: Streamline with Technology:

Look for scalable and automated business ideas that can be streamlined using technology. This allows you to reduce the time required for manual tasks and focus on essential aspects of the business.

For instance, creating and selling digital products like e-books or online courses.

3. Market Research for Target Niche: Tailor Your Services:

Conduct market research to identify a target market or niche that has demand but limited competition. Understand customer needs, preferences, and purchasing behavior. This will help you tailor your product or service effectively.

For example, if you discover a growing interest in eco-friendly products, you could start an online store specializing in sustainable home goods.

4. A Simple Business Plan: Roadmap for Success

Develop a simple business plan outlining your goals,

target market, revenue streams, and marketing strategies. A concise roadmap will help keep you organized and focused on the essential aspects of your business.

5.   Utilize E-commerce and Digital Marketing:

Utilize e-commerce platforms, social media, and digital marketing to reach a wider audience without significant time investment. Consider leveraging platforms like Amazon, Etsy, or Shopify to sell your products or services. You could also explore affiliate marketing, where you earn a commission for promoting other people's products.

6.   6. Automate Business Operations: Save Time with Technology

Streamline your business operations by automating order processing, customer service, inventory management, and marketing tasks. Take advantage of software tools and automation platforms to save time and effort.

For example, use customer relationship management

(CRM) software to manage customer interactions and automate email marketing campaigns.

7.   7. Outsource and Focus on Core Aspects

Delegate non-essential tasks by hiring virtual assistants, freelancers, or contractors to handle administrative tasks, content creation, customer support, or bookkeeping. This way, you can focus on the core aspects of your business.

8.   Prioritize Your Time and Stay Organized

Optimize your time management by setting clear priorities and allocating specific blocks of time for your business. Use productivity tools and calendars to stay organized and ensure progress on essential tasks.

For example, establish a consistent schedule for responding to customer inquiries or updating your website.

9.   Generate Passive Income Streams: Explore Opportunities

Explore opportunities for generating passive income. Consider investments, creating digital products that can be sold repeatedly, earning royalties from intellectual property, or participating in affiliate marketing programs.

10. Scale Gradually: Balance Workload and Grow Sustainably

Start small and gradually scale your business as it gains traction. Begin with a manageable workload that allows you to balance your day job and business effectively. You can gradually expand your operations by generating more income and gaining experience.

Remember that regular monitoring and maintenance are necessary even with a low-maintenance business. Allocate some time initially to set up the business, and periodically review and adjust your strategies to ensure continued success.

THE POWER OF INVESTMENTS FOR ENTREPRENEURIAL GROWTH

Entrepreneurs who juggle a day job alongside their business venture often find investments essential due to the financial resources they provide for starting and growing a business.

1. Capital For Business Operations:

Starting a business requires capital to cover various expenses such as purchasing inventory, renting office space, hiring employees, and marketing. Investments can provide the necessary funds to get the business off the ground and keep it running until it becomes self-sustaining.

For instance, imagine an entrepreneur who wants to open a boutique clothing store. Investments can help cover expenses like purchasing inventory, renting a storefront, hiring sales staff, and implementing marketing strategies. These funds are crucial to kickstarting the business and sustaining its operations until it generates sufficient revenue.

2. Scaling And Expansion:

As the business grows, additional capital may be needed to scale operations and expand into new markets. Investments can provide the financial resources required to hire more staff, invest in new equipment or technology, open new locations, or develop new products or services.

Consider a tech startup that has gained traction and wants to expand into new markets. Additional capital is needed to support the growth. Investments can provide the necessary financial resources to hire more software engineers, invest in advanced technology, establish regional offices, or diversify product offerings. This infusion of funds enables the business to capitalize on opportunities and reach a broader customer base.

3. Time Management:

Balancing a day job with entrepreneurial endeavors can be challenging. Investments can help alleviate financial pressures and allow entrepreneurs to reduce their working hours or transition to working on their business full-time. Entrepreneurs can focus more on their business growth and development with sufficient investment support.

If you're an entrepreneur who dreams of running your restaurant but currently has a day job, obtaining investments can help ease financial pressures. With the added financial support, you can reduce your working hours and dedicate more time and effort to building and growing your business (menu development and customer experience). This can help you become a successful restaurant owner and bring your vision to life."

4.   Professional Development And Education:

Investments can be used to acquire knowledge and skills through workshops, courses, mentorship programs, or industry conferences. Continual learning and professional development are crucial for entrepreneurs to stay updated with the demands of the business.

Let's say an entrepreneur runs an e-commerce business but wants to enhance their marketing skills. Investments can be used to attend digital marketing workshops, enroll in SEO and social media advertising courses, or seek mentorship from experienced marketers. By investing in their professional development, entrepreneurs can stay current on industry trends, acquire new knowledge, and apply effective business strategies.

5. Risk Mitigation:

Entrepreneurship involves a certain level of risk. Investments can help mitigate these risks by providing a financial cushion, ensuring that the entrepreneur has the necessary resources to navigate challenges, handle unexpected expenses, or survive in case of any setbacks.

Every entrepreneurial endeavor carries risks. Imagine a small business owner facing unexpected expenses or market fluctuations. Investments act as a financial cushion, providing a safety net to navigate challenges and unforeseen circumstances. They ensure the entrepreneur has the necessary resources to address setbacks, maintain business continuity, and weather uncertain times.

6. Attracting Investors And Lenders:

Having some initial investments in your business can make it more attractive to potential investors or lenders. When others see that you have already committed your resources, they may be more willing to invest or provide additional funding. #repetition

When an entrepreneur has made initial investments in their business, it demonstrates their commitment and confidence. For example, a tech startup that has secured seed funding is more likely to attract additional investments or secure loans from banks. Other investors or lenders may be more inclined to support the business when they see that the entrepreneur has already put their resources at stake.

It's vital for entrepreneurs to carefully plan and consider their financial needs and the potential returns on investments. Additionally, seeking advice from professionals, such as financial advisors or business mentors, can help make informed investment decisions.

EXPLORING AND UTILIZING PASSIVE INCOME STREAMS:

Passive income refers to earnings generated with minimal effort or ongoing involvement once the initial work or investment has been completed.

Entrepreneurs with day jobs can pursue passive income streams to supplement their earnings and create financial stability. Here's how you can look for and utilize passive income streams to generate more income:

1. Rental Income:

Entrepreneurs can invest in real estate properties and generate passive income through rental payments. For instance, purchasing a residential property and renting it out to tenants can provide a steady income stream. Other options include investing in commercial properties, vacation rentals, or parking spaces.

2. Dividend Stocks:

Investing in dividend-paying stocks allows entrepreneurs to earn passive income through regular dividend payments. Companies that distribute a portion of their profits to shareholders typically offer dividends. Entrepreneurs can benefit from steady income without active involvement by investing in stable, reputable dividend stocks.

3. Peer-to-Peer Lending:

Platforms for peer-to-peer lending connect borrowers with lenders, allowing entrepreneurs to earn passive income by lending their money to individuals or businesses. Through these platforms, entrepreneurs can diversify their investments and earn interest on the loans they provide.

4. Royalties:

You can earn passive income through royalties if you possess creative talents or intellectual property. For example, a musician can earn royalties from streaming, selling, or licensing music for commercial use. Similarly, authors can receive royalties from book sales, and inventors can earn royalties from licensing their patented technology.

5. Affiliate Marketing:

You can leverage your online presence by engaging in affiliate marketing. By promoting products or services through their website, blog, or social media platforms, entrepreneurs earn a commission for every sale or referral made through their affiliate links. This will allow you to generate passive income while continuing your day job.

6.   Digital Products:

Creating and selling digital products like e-books, online courses, or software allows entrepreneurs to earn passive income.

Once the product is developed and marketed, entrepreneurs can continue generating sales revenue without ongoing active participation.

7.   Automated Online Businesses:

Building an online business with automation can be a source of passive income. Examples include drop shipping stores, where entrepreneurs set up an online store and partner with suppliers who handle inventory management and shipping. Entrepreneurs can earn income without significant day-to-day involvement through effective marketing and automation.

Before investing your time and money in a project, conducting thorough research, seeking expert advice, and carefully considering the risks and rewards associated with each passive income opportunity is essential.

With strategic planning and the suitable investments, you can generate additional income streams that work alongside your day jobs.

In conclusion, starting a business as an entrepreneur can be challenging and uncertain, but it allows individuals to explore their abilities and create new sources of income. Maintaining a day job alongside a business can provide stability while saving money for further investment.

Regardless of the reason for starting a business, everyone must try it at least once. By following the steps outlined in this book, such as choosing a low-maintenance business model, embracing scalable ideas, conducting market research, and utilizing e-commerce and digital marketing, individuals can create a business that generates extra income and aligns with their regular employment.

Investments are crucial in providing financial resources for starting and growing a business, supporting business operations, scaling and expanding, managing time, facilitating professional development, mitigating risks, and attracting additional investors or lenders.

Furthermore, exploring and utilizing passive income streams, such as rental income, dividend stocks, peer-to-peer lending, royalties, affiliate marketing, digital products, and automated online businesses, can supplement earnings and provide financial stability. It is essential to conduct thorough research, seek expert advice, and carefully consider the risks and rewards associated with each passive income opportunity before investing time and money.

With strategic planning and the right investments, individuals can create multiple income streams that work alongside their day jobs, leading to financial growth and independence.

NOTES

The fear of failure often leads to more failures than the actual failure itself. Instead of overthinking, just do what you want to do. Take that leap of faith and start your business, ask out that girl you like, release your music, or pursue any other dream. Two things can happen - either you succeed or you fail. But if you don't try, there's only one outcome - failure! While pursuing your dreams, you may experience setbacks and failures, but it's much better than living with a permanent sense of failure that comes with not trying at all. We all had childhood dreams, so don't let them become adulthood nightmares!

MANAGING YOUR MONEY AND EARLY RETIREMENT

08

Chapter 8

MANAGING YOUR MONEY AND EARLY RETIREMENT

———

M oney management is a critical component of our lives, often disregarded or undervalued. This chapter will help you examine the need for practical financial planning and the effects of ineffective money management.

This chapter also offers advice on how to handle your finances wisely. Gaining financial freedom calls for self-control and requires a calculated strategy. This chapter dives into doable budgeting, saving, and investing methods to give you the power to take charge of your financial future and confidently pursue your objectives.

I also understand the appeal of early retirement and the desire to be free from the restrictions imposed by conventional job schedules. This chapter discusses taking advantage of compound interest and wise financial decisions to retire early.

By setting out on a path to financial independence, you can live a life of freedom and pursue your passions without being constrained by a typical career.

BUILDING A STRONG FINANCIAL FOUNDATION; EFFECTIVE BUDGETING:

Proper management of your finances holds immense importance due to various reasons:

1. Ensures Financial Stability:

Adequate financial management is essential for ensuring financial stability and security. It enables you to cover your living expenses, save for the future, and handle unexpected emergencies without accumulating debt or experiencing financial stress.

By establishing an emergency fund and saving for the future, you can better handle unexpected events such as loss of employment, medical expenses, or car repairs without experiencing significant financial setbacks.

For instance, having an emergency fund can provide a safety net to cover unforeseen medical bills or car repair costs. It can even help you navigate through periods of unemployment without facing financial hardship.

2. Helps Accomplish Goals:

Effective financial management plays a crucial role in accomplishing your goals. Whether it involves saving for a home down payment, starting a business, or planning for retirement, adeptly managing your finances allows you to allocate resources effectively and progress toward these objectives.

For instance, by carefully budgeting and saving, you can accumulate the necessary funds for a down payment on a house.

3. Minimizing Debt:

It is essential to manage your finances effectively to avoid excessive debt and make progress in paying off what you owe. Uncontrolled debt can lead to burdensome financial obligations and high-interest payments. You can achieve this by creating a budget, monitoring expenses, and reducing unnecessary debt. For instance, paying off your credit card balances monthly and refraining from excessive loans will help you keep your debt under control and save money on interest payments.

4. Relieves Financial Stress:

Taking control of your finances brings a sense of calm and peace of mind. When you clearly understand your expenses, maintain a budget, and grasp your financial situation. This helps reduce the stress and anxiety associated with money, allowing you to focus on other aspects of your life. For example, having sufficient savings to cover your monthly expenses eases worries and provides a greater sense of security.

5.   Fosters Growth Opportunities:

Thorough financial management opens avenues for investment opportunities, career advancement, and personal growth. With a solid financial foundation, you have the resources to pursue new ventures, take calculated risks, and seize potential opportunities that align with your goals.

For instance, savings and investments can provide the capital needed to start a business or take advantage of investment opportunities.

6.   Retirement Planning:

Planning for retirement is a crucial aspect of financial management. By saving and investing early, you can build a retirement nest egg that ensures financial security and allows you to enjoy your later years comfortably. For example, initiating a retirement savings plan early in your career gives your investments more time to grow, guaranteeing a stable income during retirement.

7. Achieving Financial Independence:

Effective financial management empowers you to attain financial independence, allowing you to make choices and live on your terms without financial constraints or relying on others for support. Through diligent saving and expense management, you can achieve the financial independence necessary to pursue your passions and make decisions based on personal fulfillment rather than financial limitations.

IMPACTS OF POOR MONEY MANAGEMENT:

Proper management of your finances plays a critical role in ensuring personal and financial well-being, providing many benefits, and creating opportunities for a brighter future.

In contrast, inadequate money handling can significantly affect an individual's financial well-being and overall quality of life. Here are several common consequences, accompanied by general examples:

1. Accumulation of Debt:

Managing finances often leads to excessive debt, such as credit card debt or loans. Overspending, delayed payments, or reliance on high-interest borrowing can quickly result in a cycle of debt.

For instance, consistently spending beyond one's means and making only minimum credit card payments can lead to a growing balance and increased interest charges, making it difficult to escape the debt cycle.

2. Financial Stress:

Mishandling money creates financial stress, negatively impacting mental and emotional well-being. Constant worry about bills, living paycheck to paycheck, or facing the risk of bankruptcy can result in anxiety, depression, and strained relationships.

For example, poor budgeting that prevents covering basic living expenses can cause ongoing stress and a feeling of helplessness.

3. Inability to Achieve Financial Goals:

Without proper money management, it becomes challenging to accomplish financial goals such as purchasing a house, saving for retirement, or starting a business. Insufficient savings and inefficient spending habits can delay or prevent the realization of these aspirations.

For instance, consistently overspending on non-essential items instead of saving for a down payment can prolong the process of buying a home.

4. Limited Emergency Preparedness:

Inadequate money management often leaves individuals unprepared for unexpected expenses or emergencies. Without an emergency fund or sufficient savings, people may resort to high-cost borrowing or deplete their assets.

For example, a lack of savings can make it difficult to cover medical bills resulting from unforeseen illnesses or injuries.

5. Restricted Opportunities for Wealth Building:

Inefficient money management can impede wealth accumulation and financial growth, limiting the ability to invest, seize opportunities, or build long-term assets.

For instance, consistently overspending on discretionary items instead of investing in stocks or initiating a retirement account can hinder the potential for wealth creation.

6. Limited Financial Security:

Poor money management renders individuals more vulnerable to financial hardships. Without adequate planning, they become more susceptible to economic downturns, job losses, and unforeseen bills, which can have severe repercussions.

For example, if someone unexpectedly loses their job without an emergency fund, they may struggle to meet financial obligations and risk foreclosure or eviction.

7. Poor Credit History:

Misuse of credit and debt can lead to poor credit

scores and bad credit histories. Late payments, defaults on obligations, or bankruptcy filings can make it challenging to obtain credit in the future or secure loans at reasonable interest rates. For instance, repeatedly skipping loan payments can result in a poor credit score, making it difficult to find affordable mortgage or auto financing.

It is important to note that these effects are hypothetical and may not apply universally. However, they provide a comprehensive understanding of the potential consequences of poor money management. To prevent such outcomes, it is crucial to establish sound financial practices, including budgeting, saving, and making wise purchasing decisions.

STRATEGIES FOR FINANCIAL SUCCESS:

Effectively managing your finances is vital for attaining financial stability and accomplishing your monetary objectives. Here are some approaches to financial management that will help you set yourself up for success:

1. Create A Budget:

Develop a budget to monitor your income and expenses. Allocate your money wisely by categorizing expenditures such as housing, transportation, groceries, entertainment, and savings. Utilize tools like spreadsheets or budgeting apps for organizations.

2. Save And Establish An Emergency Fund:

Set aside a portion of your income for savings and create an emergency fund. Aim to save at least 10-20% of your monthly earnings. Consider automating savings through automatic transfers to a separate savings account. For example, open a high-yield savings account and arrange automatic transfers from your checking account.

3. Minimize Debt:

Prioritize the repayment of high-interest debts like credit card debt or personal loans. Whenever possible, make payments exceeding the minimum amount to save on interest.

Explore options like debt consolidation or refinancing to lower interest rates or manage payments more effectively.

4.   Monitor And Regulate Expenses:

Keep track of your expenditures to identify areas where you can cut back. Assess your spending habits and eliminate unnecessary expenses. For instance, if you frequently eat out, try cooking at home more often or bringing lunch to work.

5.   Establish Financial Goals:

Set both short-term and long-term financial goals. Define what you wish to achieve, such as saving for a house down payment, starting a business, or retiring comfortably. Break down these goals into smaller, actionable steps.

For example, if you aim to save for a down payment, set a target amount and calculate the monthly savings required to reach that goal.

6.   Invest Wisely:

Consider investing as a means to grow your wealth

160

over time. Research various investment options, such as stocks, bonds, mutual funds, or real estate, based on your risk tolerance and financial goals.

If you lack experience in investing, seek guidance from a financial advisor or conduct thorough research before making investment decisions.

7. Review And Adjust Regularly:

Periodically evaluate your financial situation and modify your strategies as needed. Circumstances change, and your financial plan should adapt accordingly.

Monitor your budget, track progress toward your goals, and make necessary adjustments.

STRATEGIES TO ENSURE EARLY RETIREMENT:

It is always important to remember that everyone's financial situation is unique, so it is crucial to customize these strategies to suit your specific needs and objectives.

161

To attain early retirement and financial security, it is crucial to integrate disciplined savings, intelligent investments, and meticulous budgeting. While everyone's financial situation is unique, here are some overall suggestions and examples to assist you in saving money and progressing toward your goals:

1. Establish a Budget:

Start by tracking your income and expenses to understand your spending patterns better. Allocate your income toward essential expenses (e.g., housing, utilities, groceries), savings, and investments. Identify areas where you can reduce costs and increase savings.

For instance, if your monthly income is $4,000, you may assign 50% ($2,000) to essential expenses, 20% ($800) to savings, and 30% ($1,200) to discretionary spending. Adjust these percentages according to your specific circumstances.

2. Reduce Expenditures:

Evaluate your daily expenses and identify areas where you can trim costs. Analyze your spending habits and find opportunities for adjustments. Consider downsizing to a smaller home or apartment to save on mortgage or rent payments. Alternatively, you could explore options like house hacking (renting out a portion of your home) or living with roommates to split costs.

For example, you can eliminate unnecessary subscriptions, cook meals at home instead of eating out frequently, utilize public transportation or carpool instead of owning a car, take advantage of discounts and promotions while shopping, and adopt energy-saving habits to lower utility bills.

3. Save and Invest:

Build an emergency fund to cover unforeseen expenses, then focus on long-term savings and investments. Explore various investment options like stocks, bonds, mutual funds, or real estate based on your risk tolerance and financial objectives. Minimizing transportation costs by using public transit, cycling, or walking whenever possible will help you increase your savings significantly. If you need a car, consider purchasing a reliable used vehicle instead of a brand-new one to save on depreciation and insurance costs.

Consider saving a specific percentage of your monthly income, such as 20%. If your monthly income is $4,000, this would mean saving $800 per month toward long-term goals like retirement or early retirement.

4. Automate Savings:

Simplify the saving process by automatically transferring your paycheck to your savings or investment accounts. This way, a portion of your income goes directly toward your savings goals before you have the opportunity to spend it.

For example, arrange with your bank to transfer $200 from your paycheck to your retirement account every month without manual intervention.

5. Minimize Debt:

Effectively manage and reduce your debt load. Prioritize paying off high-interest debts, such as credit card balances, and consider consolidating loans to obtain lower interest rates.

For instance, if you have multiple credit cards with

outstanding balances, create a plan to pay off the card with the highest interest rate first while making minimum payments on the others.

6. Increase Income:

Explore opportunities to boost your income, such as taking on a side job, freelancing, negotiating a raise at your current job, or acquiring new skills that enhance your marketability.

If you possess a particular skill or talent, you could offer your services as a freelancer or consultant in your spare time to generate additional income.

7. Plan for Healthcare Expenses:

Keep in mind that healthcare costs can significantly impact your retirement savings. Research and understand the options available to you, such as health insurance plans and retirement healthcare savings accounts.

8. Stay Focused and Remain Flexible:

Be persistent and committed to your financial goals. Be prepared to adjust your plans as circumstances change, and stay adaptable to market conditions and economic fluctuations.

Expand your knowledge of personal finance, investment strategies, and retirement planning. Stay updated on economic trends and seek advice from financial experts or professionals as needed.

For instance, you can read books on personal finance, follow reputable financial blogs or podcasts, attend financial planning workshops, or consult a financial advisor to gain guidance and insights.

Remember that achieving early retirement and financial stability demands discipline, patience, and long-term planning. These suggestions are general, so adapting them to suit your specific circumstances and financial goals is vital while regularly reassessing and refining your strategy as you progress toward early retirement.

Effective money management is vital in our lives and should never be underestimated or overlooked. This chapter has emphasized the significance of practical financial planning and the consequences that poor money management can bring. By following this advice, you can control your finances, achieve financial freedom, and confidently pursue your goals.

You can build a solid financial foundation by implementing appropriate budgeting, saving, and investing practices. This foundation will enable you to attain financial stability, fulfill your objectives, cover living expenses, handle unexpected situations, reduce debt, alleviate financial stress, and create growth and wealth accumulation opportunities. Furthermore, early retirement planning establishes a solid groundwork for a comfortable and secure future.

By implementing the discussed strategies and maintaining discipline, patience, and adaptability, you can establish a solid financial future, achieve early retirement if desired, and enjoy the benefits of financial security and independence. Your financial well-being is within reach, and by following the steps outlined in this chapter, you can embark on a journey toward a brighter and more fulfilling financial future.

NOTES

Many people make the mistake of thinking that money is wealth. However, this is not true. Jobs can generate money, but they cannot create wealth. When you leave your job, you stop earning money. But if you have investments, you don't have to work to make money. This is true wealth! It's important to understand that money can lose its value due to devaluation, inflation, recession, and government policies. But wealth, on the other hand, can be recalculated to reflect the current market conditions. Investing in Gold is a great option as it has retained its value since creation. You don't necessarily have to invest in physical gold, you can invest in a Gold ETF. There are other investment options too, such as high-yield savings accounts and CDs that can help offset the effects of inflation. Funds can be an affordable way to diversify and invest in bundles of stocks or bonds. Government and corporate bonds can provide a source of income and cushion stock market volatility.

CONCLUSION

09

Chapter 9
CONCLUSION

As we end this journey together, let's take a moment to reflect on the key lessons learned throughout this book. We began with the realization that we all have precious time outside of our 9-to-5 jobs, and with the right strategies, we can harness that time to create multiple income streams and pursue our passions without jeopardizing our careers.

In this book, we explored the importance of negotiation and time management, which helps you achieve your fullest potential. By negotiating with our employers and using our free time wisely, we can create a balance that allows us to work on our entrepreneurial interests while maintaining productivity at our jobs. Remember, just a few extra hours a week dedicated to your side business can lead to significant progress over time.

As we delved further into entrepreneurship, we discussed the various types of businesses, emphasizing the value of product-based ventures over services. We outlined the steps to start a business: crafting a solid business plan, assessing finances, building a team, finding vendors, and setting up the legal framework. The key takeaway was to balance enthusiasm and rational decision-making regarding business development.

Another aspect we discussed was looking for ideas and side businesses that can be started alongside a day job and require minimal effort. The possibilities are vast, and you can unlock additional income streams while pursuing your passions with the right approach. Some business ideas you can seek to add an extra stream of income to your life are as follows:

1. State and Federal Procurement:

State and Federal e-procurement, or electronic procurement, revolutionizes how government agencies purchase goods and services. Agencies manage procurement more efficiently through digital platforms, such as online marketplaces and e-bidding systems. This method fosters transparency, cuts costs, and allows suppliers to bid electronically.

As a business idea, eProcurement taps into a growing market with opportunities for innovation. It addresses agencies' need for efficiency, compliance, and cost-effectiveness. Although competitive, it offers long-term contracts and stability. Success in this field demands understanding government regulations and staying abreast of policy and tech changes.

2. Internet-Based Jobs:

Embrace the digital age with online opportunities, such as freelancing in content writing, graphic design, or virtual assisting. These roles can be performed remotely and provide flexibility in managing your time. For example, As a freelance writer, you can offer your writing services to businesses and publications, creating engaging content and articles.

3. Managing an Amazon Online Store:

Leverage the booming e-commerce industry by setting up your own Amazon store. Choose products that align with your interests and cater to a specific niche market. For instance, If you are passionate about fitness, you can start an Amazon store selling fitness equipment and accessories.

4. Book Writing:

Unleash your creativity and share your knowledge by becoming an author or self-publisher. Whether fiction, non-fiction, or educational material, writing a book can open up new opportunities. For example, If you are knowledgeable about personal finance, you can write a book offering practical financial advice to readers.

5. Working as a Transcriptionist:

If you possess strong listening and typing skills, transcription work can be a reliable source of income.

You can transcribe audio files for various clients and industries. Medical transcriptionists convert medical records and dictations into written reports, serving healthcare professionals.

6.   Start a Blog:

Share your expertise, experiences, or passions through blogging and monetize them through advertisements or affiliate marketing. A well-maintained blog can generate passive income over time.

If you are a travel enthusiast, you can start a travel blog and share your adventures, travel tips, and destination reviews.

7.   Explore Content Writing:

If you have a way with words, freelance writing can be a lucrative side gig, creating content for various clients.

You can write blog posts, articles, or social media content for businesses and individuals looking to improve their online presence.

8.   Try Web Design Services:

If you know how to design websites, utilize your web design skills to create stunning websites for individuals or small businesses looking to establish an online presence.

You can offer web design services to local startups or entrepreneurs who need a professional business website.

9.   Try Content Creation:

Engage an audience with your video content on a YouTube channel and monetize it through advertisements and sponsorships. Trying to create content is also a very low-investment business idea, as all you need to start is your phone camera and your creativity. For example, if you have a passion for cooking, you can start a cooking channel where you share delicious recipes and culinary tips.

After establishing an online presence, you can also collaborate with brands you love and represent them as a brand ambassador, promoting their products or services. For instance, If you are a fitness enthusiast, you can partner with fitness brands to promote their products on social media.

10. Try Online Teaching:

Share your knowledge and skills in a specific subject by becoming a tutor for students of all ages.

If you know languages, you can utilize your language skills by becoming an online language tutor and connecting with students worldwide. For instance, if you are fluent in Spanish, you can teach Spanish lessons to language learners of all ages.

11. Declutter your Life:

Declutter your space and earn extra cash by selling used items on platforms like eBay or Craigslist. You can sell vintage clothing and accessories you no longer use but are in good condition.

12. Staging Homes for Real Estate:

Help sellers showcase their properties in the best light by providing home staging services and assisting real estate agents in attracting potential buyers. You can work with a real estate agent to stage a home for sale with furniture and decor highlighting its features.

13. Providing Financial Services:

If you have a background in finance, consider offering financial consulting or planning services to individuals seeking guidance. You can use your experience to provide personalized financial advice to young professionals looking to invest wisely and plan for their future.

14. Pet Sitting:

Animal lovers can earn extra income by offering pet-sitting or dog-walking services to busy pet owners who need help caring for their pets. You can start pet sitting by providing services to pet owners in your neighborhood, ensuring their furry friends receive attentive care.

You can also combine your love for pets with a side business by offering dog-walking services in your neighborhood. You can offer daily dog-walking services to busy pet owners who may not have time to walk their dogs regularly.

15. Become a Rideshare Driver:

Use your car to become a rideshare driver and earn money during your spare time by giving rides to passengers. To start, you can join a rideshare platform and offer transportation services to people within your city or town.

16. Running Errands for People:

Offer errand services to individuals needing assistance with grocery shopping or picking up dry cleaning. You can run errands for busy professionals with limited time for personal tasks during their workweek or those struggling with their mental or physical health and needing assistance completing their daily tasks. This will not only help you earn more money, but it will also help you form stronger bonds in your community.

17. Try Monetizing Your Hobbies:

Tap into your creative side by making and selling crafts, art, or handmade products. If you are skilled in pottery, you can create unique and artistic pottery pieces to market online or at local craft fairs. You can also monetize your skills around the house, like painting walls or fixing small leaks around the neighborhood. You can offer interior or exterior house painting services to homeowners looking to refresh their property's look.

18. Become a Mystery Shopper:

You can get paid to visit and evaluate various establishments, providing valuable feedback to businesses about their customer service and operations. As a mystery shopper, you can visit restaurants, rate the service and food quality, and be paid for it.

19. Take Online Surveys:

You can participate in online surveys and market research studies to earn extra cash by providing valuable consumer insights. For example, you can join survey platforms and complete product preference surveys and lifestyle habits.

20. Online Coaching and Motivational Speaking:

Share your expertise and inspire others through online coaching or motivational speaking, guiding individuals toward personal growth and success.

As a certified life coach, you can offer virtual coaching sessions to clients seeking guidance in achieving their goals.

Remember the significance of negotiating with your current employer in pursuing side business opportunities. Many employers are open to their employees exploring side ventures as long as they don't conflict with the company's interests or create competition. Effective communication and transparency are vital in reaching a mutually beneficial agreement.

Combine the potential of side businesses with robust negotiation strategies to pave your way toward financial freedom and early retirement. Embrace the thrilling journey ahead and seize the chance to shape your future.

Marketing is critical for any business's success. A well-thought-out marketing plan is essential to reach potential customers and establish connections effectively. This plan should encompass a situation analysis, competitor research, objectives, strategies, target audience, and action plans.

As we learn the tips and tricks to grow our businesses, we discover the importance of establishing independent systems. These systems allow us to invest our time and resources in other areas while generating passive income.

Money management plays a pivotal role in our journey to financial freedom. By implementing intelligent financial practices like budgeting, saving, and wise investing, we secure our future and unlock the door to early retirement.

Early retirement is not merely about leaving work; it's

about gaining the freedom to choose how we spend our time. This liberty empowers us to pursue our passions, explore new interests, and positively impact the world on our terms.

Upon achieving early retirement, one often finds ample free time and financial security, enabling individuals to explore various activities and pursue their passions with newfound freedom. Here are some positive examples of things people can do after early retirement.

1. Travel the World:

With no work commitments holding them back, early retirees can embark on exciting journeys to explore different cultures, landscapes, and cuisines. They can indulge in immersive travel experiences and create lasting memories.

2. Volunteer for Causes You Care About:

Early retirees can dedicate their time and skills to charitable organizations or community projects. This allows them to give back to society and make a positive impact on the lives of others.

Having financial stability, early retirees can become philanthropists and support causes they are passionate about. They can donate to charitable organizations or establish charitable **foundations to impact society positively.**

3. Pursue Hobbies and Interests:

Whether it's painting, playing a musical instrument, gardening, writing, or photography, early retirement offers the opportunity to delve deep into hobbies and interests previously limited by time constraints.

4. Focus on Your Health:

Early retirees have more time to focus on their physical and mental well-being. They can exercise regularly, take fitness classes, practice yoga, or participate in outdoor activities, contributing to a healthier lifestyle.

5. Start a Small Business or Side Project:

With financial security in place, some early retirees start a small business or work on a side project that aligns with their passions and interests. It could be anything from an online store to consulting services.

6. Spend Quality Time with Family and Friends:

Early retirement allows individuals to strengthen their bonds with loved ones. They can spend more time with their children, grandchildren, and friends, creating cherished memories.

7. Learn New Skills:

Retirement doesn't mean the end of learning. Early retirees can take courses or workshops to learn new skills, whether a new language, cooking techniques, or computer programming.

8. Focus on Personal Development:

Early retirement is an excellent time for self-reflection and personal growth. Individuals can improve their emotional intelligence, communication skills, or other areas they wish to develop.

9. Spend Time in Nature:

Exploring the outdoors, hiking in nature reserves, camping, or enjoying peaceful moments in natural settings can become a regular part of your lifestyle once you fulfill your early retirement dreams, fostering a deeper connection with the environment.

10. Join Social Clubs or Groups:

You can join social clubs or interest groups catering to their hobbies and passions, allowing you to meet like-minded individuals and form new friendships.

11. Mentor or Coach Others:

After gaining valuable experience throughout their career, early retirees can share their knowledge by becoming mentors or coaches, guiding younger generations to achieve their goals.

It also offers the time and space for creative expression. Some retirees may write a book or start a blog to share their experiences, knowledge, and stories with the world.

12. Embrace Slow Living:

With no hectic work schedule, early retirees can adopt a slower and more intentional way of living. They can savor everyday moments and focus on living in the present. They have enough time on their hands to explore museums and art galleries, attend concerts, and engage in cultural activities, deepening their appreciation for the arts.

Remember, these are just general examples, and each person's journey will be unique based on their interests and aspirations. The key is to make the most of the newfound freedom and embrace a fulfilling and purposeful life beyond the traditional work years.

Throughout this book, I have shared my experiences and knowledge, hoping to inspire you to take charge of your life, balance your career with your entrepreneurial aspirations, and strive for financial independence. I am grateful for the opportunity to have been your guide on this transformative journey.

As you embark on your path to financial freedom and early retirement, remember there will always be challenges. Still, you can overcome any obstacle with determination, perseverance, and a strategic mindset.

Embrace continuous learning, seek advice from mentors, and surround yourself with like-minded individuals who share your vision.

May you find fulfillment in every endeavor, and may your future be filled with purpose, joy, and the satisfaction of living on your terms. Your journey to financial freedom has just begun, and I do not doubt you will achieve greatness.

Remember, the power to design the life you desire lies within you. Embrace it, live it, and enjoy the fruits of your labor.

Here's to your success and a life well lived!

NOTES

Become a ghost for a year. Leave your hometown where everybody knows you from your past. Use the absence to increase your worth. But don't depend on absence alone. Rely also on personal development. Increase your value by being scarce. Improve your body by working out. Increase your net worth by networking. Increase your indispensability by learning new cutting-edge skills. Expand your vocabulary by reading. Words have power. And the more words you know, the more power you have. Eloquence leads to opulence. Focus on self-discovery, self-improvement, and self-discipline. Then, resurrect as a new and improved version of you that adds value to any location you find yourself within the population.

If you look at the most successful musicians and artists, they use this strategy. Businesses use that strategy. Artificial scarcity creates automatic quality.

One of the greatest politicians that ever lived, Napoleon Bonaparte, said, "If I am often seen at the theatre, people will cease to notice me."

Take currency, for example. For money to have value, it must create the illusion of being scarce.

If you think your need will attract money to you, your expectations will be shattered, and the shattering may damage your health. Wealth is not a respecter of need. Wealth is a respecter of principles. Understand the principles of wealth, and you will be a principal man.

Money doesn't go where there is need. Money goes where conditions are ideal. When wealth finds itself in the hands of a man who understands money, it will remain there and begin to multiply. Do not focus on only what you like. Learn what money likes and do it well!

Always treat money like a hen. If you eat your hen, it is gone. But if you feed it until it lays eggs, it endures. Eat only what you need. Then, let the remaining eggs hatch into hens. You will then have multiple hens laying multiple eggs, and you will never be poor.

Look at the way God created creation. Everything you eat in nature is naturally regenerated. If you pluck an orange and eat it, you spit out the seeds, which sprout into new orange trees. Use money like that. Eat it, but spit out some to invest and yield more money!

A line has a beginning and an end. So, if you get your money from point A and immediately spend it at point B, your money will have a beginning and an end. A circle has no beginning or end. So if you get your money and you invest before spending, it will never end!

If you want your money never to finish, you must circulate it. When money comes (money comes to everybody at some point), invest it. When it yields profit, spend some and reinvest the rest. If you obey this law of circulating money, you will never be broke in life.

Life is a circle. It comes round in cycles. Everything in life that has sustainability must exist in a cycle. In physics, the sun is maintained by a solar cycle. And the moon also has a lunar cycle called a lunar phase.

A cycle is a natural phenomenon in which elemental, human, and animal creatures are moving in a continuum of maturity through various phases and forms of existence that repeat themselves and, by so doing, sustain life on Earth in a consistent pattern of growth that is in harmony with nature.

An empty pocket is usually the result of an empty mind. Even if you give money to a man with an empty mind, the money won't last. It is like pouring water into a basket. Only knowledge and wisdom can plug those holes. Know and grow. Learn and earn! In school, you only get promoted to the next class when you know too much for the class you are in. In life, you will only get promoted financially when you improve in knowledge and wisdom. Skilled workers earn favor. Unskilled workers earn labor!

www.ingramcontent.com/pod-product-compliance
Lightning Source LLC
Chambersburg PA
CBHW070656190326
41458CB00052B/6903/J